THE
RIGHT-TO-EDUCATION
CHILD

THE RIGHT-TO-EDUCATION CHILD

(A Curriculum for the Severely and Profoundly Mentally Retarded)

By

DONALD G. MYERS, Ed.D.

Associate Professor and Chairman of the Graduate Department of Special Education, Marywood College
Scranton, Pennsylvania

MICHAEL E. SINCO, M.S.

Curriculum Coordinator and Psychologist, Northeastern Educational Intermediate Unit Nineteen
Scranton, Pennsylvania

ELLEN SOMERTON STALMA, B.A.

Head Teacher, The Right to Education Program
Northeastern Educational Intermediate Unit Nineteen
Scranton, Pennsylvania

CHARLES C THOMAS · PUBLISHER
Springfield · Illinois · U.S.A.

Published and Distributed Throughout the World by
CHARLES C THOMAS • PUBLISHER
Bannerstone House
301-327 East Lawrence Avenue, Springfield, Illinois, U.S.A.

© *1973, by* CHARLES C THOMAS • PUBLISHER

ISBN 0-398-02923-7

Library of Congress Catalog Card Number: 73-8661

Library of Congress Cataloging in Publication Data

Myers, Donald G.
    The right-to-education child.

    1. Mentally handicapped children—Care and treat-
ment. 2. Mentally handicapped children—Education.
I. Sinco, Michael E., joint author. II. Stalma,
Ellen Somerton, joint author. III. Title.
[DNLM: 1. Education of mentally retarded. LC4601
M996r 1973]
RJ506.M4M9   649'.15'28   73-8661
ISBN   0-398-02923-7

Printed in the United States of America
C-1

FOREWORD

COUNTLESS NUMBERS of special education seminars purported to provide general, and even specific, applications of educative processes for exceptional children have produced broad educational philosophical methodologies and developmental steps that have been apparently (a) discovered, (b) discussed, (c) disseminated, (d) disregarded and finally (e) disremembered.

The Right-to-Education Child: A Curriculum for the Severely and Profoundly Mentally Retarded now offers an area of applied functions of the school center based around learning and motivation. Stemming from a dire need for effective applications of developmental steps dealing with aiding hundreds of mentally retarded youngsters under the jurisdiction of the Northeastern Educational Intermediate Unit, Scranton, Pennsylvania, is an educational agency totally dedicated to upgrading applicable teaching skills and is therein significantly helping youngsters.

In the preparation of this *textbook of teaching-skills*, the combined experiences and views of actively interested educators has been wisely (a) apprised, (b) absorbed, (c) acclaimed, (d) acknowledged and finally (e) accepted collectively and purposefully to help teachers of severely mentally retarded children cope with their involved multitudinous complexities.

The authors have written this book, commendably designed to answer questions dealing with *The Right-to-Education Child: A Curriculum for the Severely and Profoundly Mentally Retarded.*

The preparer of this Foreword humbly believes this document, to all its readers, should be and will be (a) creditable, (b) communicative, (c) contributory, (d) contemporary and finally (e) consumable.

P. M. MENSKY, Ed.D.
Executive Director,
Northeastern Educational
Intermediate Unit,
Scranton, Pennsylvania

PREFACE

Pᴀɪɴꜰᴜʟʟʏ sʟᴏᴡʟʏ, but inevitably, the doctrine establishing a zero reject system of free public education and training for the mentally retarded has attained the force of law in the State of Pennsylvania, with many states to follow. This doctrine demands that no school district may postpone, terminate or in any way deny the right to a program of free public education and training to any retarded child. It establishes that every retarded child can benefit from a program of education and training no matter what label, based on IQ (educable, trainable or profoundly retarded), has been applied to the child; it further requires the retarded child to be placed in a public program of education and training appropriate to the child's capacity.

The Right-to-Education Child: A Curriculum for the Severely and Profoundly Mentally Retarded represents the authors' attempt to eagerly apply themselves to the task of implementing this new educational legislation. This book will be different from most other books on education. The reader will not find any traditional or comfortable *ABC*-type educational curriculum within the book. The curriculum consists of the child with the teaching task focusing on skills such as swallowing, chewing and crawling. The authors have written this text as a result of experience gained from working with these children. It is hoped that our efforts and the knowledge we gained will result in the demystification of the abilities and limitations of the severely and profoundly retarded, with worthy and appropriate education to follow which will help these youngsters grow, rather than merely exist.

The techniques presented in this book are based on well established principles of learning. By following the step-by-step procedures carefully detailed in this book, anyone can successfully learn to teach the severely and profoundly mentally retarded.

The content of the book is based on a concrete curriculum with clear, understandable, instructional objectives; readiness suggested for success in a specific task area and procedures that are basic and direct to achieve task competency. Numerous illustrations of procedures will serve as a practical guide for the experienced or inexperienced. Resource materials are listed for further information.

This book will serve a unique role in program development and implementation. It is also intended to be used as a training text at in-service conferences. The book is restricted in its scope to problems directly related to teaching the severely and profoundly retarded. It is believed that the reader will be shown methods that will enable anyone to help these forgotten, waiting youngsters to learn self-care skills, and hopefully will lead to the development of life skills necessary for more successful functioning in our everyday society.

Donald G. Myers
Michael E. Sinco
Ellen S. Stalma

ACKNOWLEDGMENTS

W E WISH TO EXPRESS our appreciation to Paul Argenio, Assistant Director of Instructional Materials, Northeastern Educational Intermediate Unit Nineteen, Scranton, Pennsylvania, for the illustrations within the procedures, and Loraine Yuskiewicz for her graphic illustrations that appear throughout the text.

CONTENTS

	Page
Foreword	v
Preface	vii
Acknowledgments	ix

Chapter

I. INTRODUCTION	3
II. OBJECTIVES	7
III. THE CURRICULUM	17
Appendix	227
Index	229

THE
RIGHT-TO-EDUCATION
CHILD

Figure 1

(Chapter 1)

INTRODUCTION

THE AMERICAN ASSOCIATION on Mental Deficiency refers to mental retardation as subaverage intellectual functioning which originated during the developmental period and is associated with an impairment in adaptive behavior.

On an intelligence scale, the mentally retarded would be those who have an intelligence quotient of approximately *seventy and below*. This book will focus on those individuals functioning at the severe and the profound levels of mental retardation. Although such individuals are difficult to accurately measure intellectually, a rough estimate would place them on an intelligence scale at *thirty-five or below*.

It is recognized that the intelligence quotient should not be the only criterion used in making a diagnosis of mental retardation, or in evaluating its severity. It should serve only to help in making a more accurate judgment of the individual's adaptive behavioral capacity. Also, any classification system tends to lead to an oversimplification of problems that are complex and perplexing. Within each level there are wide differences of ability potentiality. For these reasons it is preferable to focus on the dimension of adaptive behavior which refers primarily to the effectiveness with which an individual copes with the natural and social demands of his environment.

In order to better understand the severely and profoundly mentally retarded, the authors offer the following brief list of descriptions that characterize such individuals:

1. Physical defects are numerous and often severe, i.e. impaired vision, hearing and mechanisms for motor coordination.
2. May or may not be ambulatory.
3. May show complete unawareness of the environment.

3

4. Often displays extreme infantile-type behavior.
5. Frequently unable to communicate or relate to others.
6. Often speech remains undeveloped although sounds are made.
7. Care of bodily functions pose serious problems, i.e. absence of feeding and toileting skills.
8. Most often cannot guard themselves against the most common physical dangers.

The great majority of our severely and profoundly retarded population can be found in state institutions or in smaller public and private facilities. Many children do remain at home for as long as the family is able to care for them. However, difficulties in care for the severely and profoundly retarded increase as the child gets older. Parents expect to give a newborn total care, seeing to his needs twenty-four hours a day. There is joy in this helping, dependency role, but the joy is often made possible by knowing that the dependent relationship is short lived. Total care of a three, five, ten or twenty-year-old individual places tremendous strain on any family unit, and the mother in particular.

The need for constant care: feeding, dressing and toileting requires an almost constant vigil. However, this is only one demanding aspect. Parents of these children often have feelings of guilt, insecurity and doubt about their ability to care for the child. Parents may even blame one another for being the possible cause of the problem. If there are other children in the family, they must make allowances for the added attention given to the *special* child. This is not always easy, depending on the age and disposition of the children who are expected to understand this most difficult situation.

Society often exerts pressures on parents to place the retarded child in an institution. A mere stare on the street, a guarded conversation by a neighbor or reluctance to visit in the home brings about a range of emotions which members of the family are not equipped to handle.

The history of the education of the severely and profoundly retarded is not very noteworthy or illustrous either, and therefore will receive limited comment. Most of the educational opportunities for the severely and profoundly retarded were found in residential schools. It was only at the turn of this century that special classes for the retarded in public school systems were initiated, and they have grown steadily since then. However, no specific program provisions were made for the severely and profoundly retarded, and they became specifically excluded from school. At this time the concept of the *uneducable,* a disgraceful term, came to be applied to the lower functioning retarded children.

An increasing number of parents and concerned citizens felt the exclusion concept to be unjust. Gradually, from about 1930 on, local parent organizations began to appear. About 1950, these groups consolidated into the National Association for Retarded Children. This group, together with a number of interested professional groups, brought the whole problem of the needs of the retarded into clearer focus. As a result of their efforts, on October 7, 1971, the doctrine establishing a *zero reject* system of free public education and training for the mentally retarded attained the force of law in the State of Pennsylvania. No longer will a school system postpone, terminate or in any way deny the mentally retarded the right to a program of free public education and training.

Although much greater public awareness of the lower functioning mentally retarded may now be observed, much remains to be accomplished in providing appropriate educational opportunities and experiences. Nevertheless, *The Right-to-Education Child* has been born.

Figure 2

(CHAPTER 2)

OBJECTIVES

IN DEVELOPING OBJECTIVES for a curriculum, it would appear that the basic philosophy should be that the severely and profoundly mentally retarded are children, and that the goal should be to help each realize his maximum potential, just as it is for every child.

In working toward adequate curriculum objectives, many aspects need to be considered. It is quite unrealistic for a teacher to offer these children experiences merely because such experiences have always been offered, or because they are the procedures the teacher knows. Each teacher must be aware of the fact that the entire educational program for the severely and profoundly retarded must be directed at developing skills in basic sensory, motor, self-care and language areas. Such skills seem essential in beginning any type of learning sequence for these children. It is also felt that the program must be highly structured, and present situations and experiences in which the stimuli to which the children are exposed are carefully controlled. Because of the strict curriculum structure, educators must be careful in teaching by the method of imitation. The children being taught will not only learn the correct, but also the incorrect methods by the imitative process. The teacher should also be careful not to respond inappropriately to an inaccurate or incorrect task performance. The child's behavior may seem cute, but such teacher behavior will usually encourage further undesired responding by the child. Always be aware of *your* behavior and then the child's.

EXPLANATION IN THE USE OF THE CURRICULUM

In today's educational process it is quite natural for teachers to participate in group work in curriculum planning and devel-

7

opment. The final translation of the curriculum guide into actual experiences for the children is the responsibility of the teacher. In the case of the severely and profoundly mentally retarded, where the classes are so few and geographically isolated, the burden of curriculum-making rests heavily on the individual teacher. Also such a teacher will have the children under his direction for a much longer period of time than is customary in the regular schools; thus the problems of scope and sequence of the program will depend solely on the specific teacher.

While each teacher generally has his own curriculum ideas and plan, the curriculum in this text offers the educator a complete and new method of teaching the severely and profoundly retarded. It is based on action-oriented programs and successful classroom use. The curriculum emphasizes experiences needed by children at a very low developmental level. A clear, logical sequence of tasks are then presented to each child. The level and sequence of the various experiences depend, to a great extent, on the readiness of the child. In most instances it will be necessary to break down the educational experiences into very basic competencies and teach these serially. The procedures in the curriculum will order the task to be taught into small manageable steps. By utilizing such an approach, it is hoped that no behavior, no matter how small or inconsequential it may seem, will be overlooked or disregarded. The teacher must be perceptive even to the child's cooing and babbling; it means something to the child. Likewise, the teacher must learn that any successes of the child will be very, very small, but most important in the process of developing the child's skill area.

The curriculum consists of units of instruction in four broad developmental areas: (1) Sensory, (2) Motor, (3) Self-Care and (4) Language. Each instructional unit will consist of: (1) Instructional Objective, (2) Readiness, (3) Procedures, (4) Task Evaluation and (5) Materials and Equipment. A brief description of each will follow.

Instructional Objective

Each objective specifies the competency to be demonstrated or the behavior the instruction is to produce. Each objective is seen as a basis for setting the dimension of the lesson and provides the format for structuring the activities, evaluating the child's performance and selecting of resources. Objectives must be well stated and designed. An instructional objective may involve the child being able to successfully chew and swallow chopped food. A situation must then be developed and structured to produce the behavior. Later, the teacher can determine whether or not the instructional objective has been met.

Readiness

Readiness is the absolute minimum behavioral competency needed to start an instructional objective. Establishing readiness levels are desired to encourage the greatest possible program flexibility. For example, if the instructional objective requires the child to successfully chew and swallow chopped food, the readiness would be that no apparent physiological impairment is present that would prevent such a behavior. The esophagus must be open sufficiently to pass solids.

Procedures

The procedures are the tasks available to the child to facilitate mastery of the instructional objective. The procedures are developmental with complex activities broken down into small, specific teaching tasks. For example, one step in the procedures for achieving the chewing and swallowing objective may require the physical manipulation of the jaws.

Task Evaluation

The evaluation process is essential in determining the successful completion of an instructional objective and improving an instructional program. In order to evaluate educational progress, the major target behavior should be day-to-day performance. For example, evaluation would determine to what extent the child was successful in chewing and swallowing chopped food.

Materials and Equipment

Most educational activities will require teaching or resource materials and equipment. Suggestions and listed items are provided that might assist the teacher in directing the instructional objectives. For example, in chewing and swallowing chopped food, meatloaf, green beans, carrots and noodles in bite size form are suggested. It must be pointed out that the vast majority of the materials and equipment used in the curriculum are readily available at nominal cost in any neighborhood variety store.

BEHAVIOR CHARTING PROCEDURES

One of the most difficult tasks for teachers to do is to list the behavioral changes they want to achieve in children. It is the behavioral charting procedures that will enable teaching personnel to observe and record the presence and degree of various types of behavioral competencies demonstrated by the severely and profoundly mentally retarded.

The competency *checklists* are useful diagnostically, prognostically and particularly for following the educational program. The checklist permits the teacher to estimate the degree of improvement in relation to further training for the child. The checklist which precedes each of the instructional units is organized according to the complexity of developmental behavior. It provides the user with a curriculum plan, a series of behavioral expectancies and activities to facilitate behavioral change. By completing the checklist before entering an instructional program, the teacher will have an accurate determination of the child's level of present functioning. This will also provide a goal and reporting system while involved in instruction.

Observing and reporting behavior is an essential part of the curriculum. Numerous charts are therefore used. A brief description of the various types of charts that may prove valuable in checking and reporting behavior will follow.

Curriculum Chart

This chart identifies eight general program areas and the competency levels established for a certain child. A bar graph at the top is used to depict the child's present level of competency ranging from zero blocks (no competency) to four blocks (complete competency). Such a visual representation of the child's level of

CURRICULUM CHART

Name: Alex

Motor Training	Toileting	Self-Feeding	Self-Washing	Oral Hygiene	Nasal Hygiene	Self-Dressing	Communication
no blocks – no attempt to move	*no blocks* – not on tt program	*no blocks* – spoon fed baby food	*no blocks* – no attempt to assist in washing self	*no blocks* – no attempt to assist in brushing teeth	*no blocks* – no attempt to clean nose	*no blocks* – no attempt to dress or un-dress self	*no blocks* – no attempt to communicate
1 block – gain head control	*1 block* – on tt program w v sporadic results	*1 block* – eats chopped food	*1 block* – attempts to wash hands at sink	*1 block* – allows his teeth to be brushed	*1 block* – aware of need to clean nose	*1 block* – removes socks	*1 block* – recognizes name
2 blocks – sits w support	*2 blocks* – eliminates during day when placed on potty	*2 blocks* – finger feeds self	*2 blocks* – tries to apply soap to wash-cloth	*2 blocks* – helps brush by using a hand over hand method	*2 blocks* – puts hand over adults when having nose cleaned	*2 blocks* – removes pants when unfast & shirt when arms released with help	*2 blocks* – attends to voice when being spoken to
3 blocks – brings self to sitting post. & sits alone	*3 blocks* – gestures toilet need	*3 blocks* – feeds self with hand over hand assistance	*3 blocks* – attempts to wash entire body in tub	*3 blocks* – brushes teeth by self	*3 blocks* – tries to clean nose by self with tissue to face	*3 blocks* – can take off pull over shirt indep.	*3 blocks* – laughs, coos, or babbles in response to stimulation
4 blocks – stands with support	*4 blocks* – begins to move-toilet unattended	*4 blocks* – feeds self independ. with spoon	*4 blocks* – attempts to dry entire body	*4 blocks* – applies tooth paste & brushes teeth by self	*4 blocks* – obtains tissue & cleans nose by self	*4 blocks* – attempts to put pants on & shirt	*4 blocks* – imitates simple gestures i.e. bye, bye or hi

Figure 3

functioning, stated in broad terms, is an aid to the teacher in readily accessing the child's needs and also his achievements. This chart is especially helpful if more than one person is involved in the instructional process.

Individual Prescription Chart

The prescription chart may be helpful by reinforcing to the teacher the child's educational program. By placing the chart on display it serves to remind and focus the teacher on the specific activities of daily living that are of concern. A prescription may be written on more than one area. The chart provides information on current level of achievement and plans procedures to increase the child's competency. In the chart below it will be noted that self-feeding was the area of immediate concern, thus the step-by-step procedures have been developed.

Educational Encounter Reporting

Several types of this report may prove useful. The *Daily Encounter Report* consists of a detailed narrative of a learning session.

INDIVIDUAL PRESCRIPTION CHART

Name	Activities of Daily Living (circle concern)	Competency	Procedures
ALEX	(Self-feeding)	Ready to begin feeding self with a spoon with hand over hand method	1. Seat Alex at feeding table 2. Sit down by him 3. Introduce bowl of food with large handled therapy spoon in it 4. Hand the empty spoon to Alex & then secure his grasp by putting your hand over his
	Self-dressing	Pulls off socks when they are at the mid foot position	
	Toileting	On tt program, but rarely eliminates on potty	
	Communication	Recognizes name & follows simple commands	5. Assist him in moving spoon into bowl & scooping food onto spoon
	Motor	Remains in a sitting position	6. Direct spoon to his mouth
	Grooming	Makes no attempt to care for self, but permits others to	7. When food is taken direct spoon back to the bowl 8. Reward verbally

Figure 4

Educational Encounter Report

Name: ALEX
Concentration Area: Self-feeding
Time Involved: 20 min.

Date: 3-20-73
Location: Eating area
Submitted: MES

PROCEDURE—I first sat Alex at the feeding table and then sat down next to him on his right. I introduced his food to him explaining that it was beef stew. I handed him the large handled therapy spoon putting my hand over his. Together we put the spoon in the bowl and scooped out a small amount. I helped Alex in putting the spoon into his mouth. He took the food as I instructed him and he returned the spoon to the bowl.

RESULTS—Alex did very well for the first half of the session. He was very interested and seemed pleased that he could be somewhat independent in feeding himself. Toward the end of the session he began to get tired and his hand kept slipping from the spoon. At this point in the session praise for his behavior was stopped.

RECOMMENDATIONS—Continued placement of Alex on the feeding program, with supplemental grasp development exercises.

The *Weekly Encounter Report* is a detailed narrative of the week's general classroom procedures and results. It serves as a self-check for the teacher, ensuring that the established educational program is implemented.

Educational Encounter Report

Name: ALEX
Concentration Area: Self-feeding

Week of: March 18, 1973
Submitted: MES

GENERAL PROCEDURES—Alex was worked with at each meal during the day this week. The majority of the food that was given to him was of the type that could be served in a bowl, such as beef stew, chili etc. The step-by-step method was followed closely. When Alex began to get tired and lax about holding the spoon, he was fed by the instructor to complete his meal.

GENERAL RESULTS—Alex certainly seems to have gained skill

this week. His grasp is much stronger and he is completing more of the meal before he tires. I have noticed that his motor development is not improving. It is still necessary for Alex to be supported while in the sitting position, at times. His head control is very good.

SPECIFIC NOTABLE EVENTS—On Wednesday morning, Alex ate his entire bowl of oatmeal without hesitation. This is particularly notable, since prior to this point he has always tired or become disruptive before finishing the meal.

RECOMMENDATIONS—1. Continued placement on feeding program. 2. Supplemental grasp development exercises. 3. Supplemental time provided for sitting with minimal support.

Toilet Training Chart

The toileting chart permits a two hour check of the child's elimination control. The factor of time is of critical importance. Significant daily remarks should be recorded.

Toilet Training Chart

Toileting Behavior   Name: ALEX

X   = no results
U   = urinated
BM   = bowel movement
Wet = wet before placed on toilet
Dry = dry before placed on toilet

Date			*Time*				*Remarks*
March	7	9	11	1	3	5	
13	wet	dry	wet	dry	wet	wet	had one success; was dry
	X	U	X	X	X	X	when put on toilet
14	wet	wet	wet	wet	wet	wet	went entire day without
	X	X	X	X	X	X	a success on the toilet
15	dry	wet	wet	wet	wet	dry	made a BM in toilet and
	U	X	U	X	X	BM	was able to urinate twice

16	wet	wet	dry	wet	wet	wet	had two successes on the
	X	X	U	U	X	BM, X	toilet
17	wet	dry	dry	wet	wet	dry	was dry more today, and had two successes on the
	X	U	X	X	X	U	toilet

Happenings Chart

This chart is very helpful in any learning environment. The *happenings chart* provides a teacher with a means of communicating to others *unexpected* successes and accomplishments of the children. It adds a new dimension of perceptiveness to the teacher's role, making each an alert observer of new and changing behavior.

Happenings Chart

A happening is a wonderful thing . . . the first time a child does or says something . . . new!

Mike K.	1-22-73	9:00 A.M. took spoonful of food himself and returned spoon to the bowl.
Darryl B.	2-16-73	4:00 P.M. turned head in direction of loud noise made to his right side.
Maggie K.	3-11-73	8:30 A.M. rolled from her stomach to her back.
Karen R.	3-26-73	12:30 P.M. pulled feet from basin of cold water while being stimulated with warm and cold water.

Chapter 3

THE CURRICULUM

Figure 5

UNIT I
SENSORY DEVELOPMENT

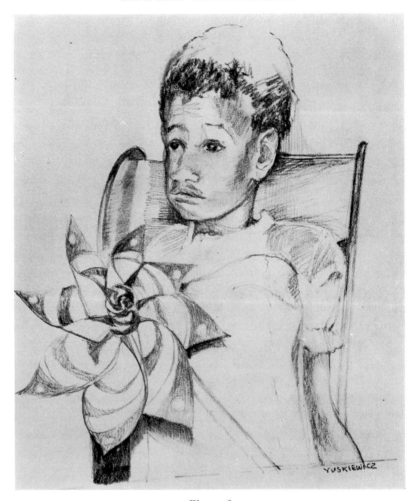

Figure 6

Competency Checklist

Name _____   Educational Facility _____

Date _____   Educator _____

Instructional Unit
Sensory Development

Code:

0 No Competency
1 Moderate Competency
2 Complete Competency

.... 1. Permits directed body movements.
.... 2. Responds to vibrator stimulation.
.... 3. Responds to brushing stimulation.
.... 4. Responds to icing stimulation.
.... 5. Responds to warm and cold water stimulation.
.... 6. Responds to hair dryer stimulation.
.... 7. Discriminates between various types of tactile stimulation.
.... 8. Responds to auditory stimulation.
.... 9. Responds to visual stimulation.
.... 10. Responds to olfactory stimulation.
.... 11. Responds to taste stimulation.
.... Total (max. 22)
Remarks:

Instructional Objective

To direct the child's body into a variety of positions, in order to stimulate muscles and circulatory processes.

Readiness

No apparent physiological impairment that would prevent or inhibit response to body manipulation.

No physical disability that would be complicated by body rolling and manipulation.

Procedure

1. This exercise is designed to stimulate through the use of body manipulation.

2. Various types of equipment can be used in the manipulation of the body. Some are: bean bag chairs, large beach balls, large cardboard tubes and a mattress or soft carpet.

3. The use of the bean bag chair proves quite rewarding for the nonambulatory child who has limited movement. The chair conforms to the shape of the child and he can be safely situated in a variety of positions while in the chair.

4. The large beach ball should be large enough to accommodate the entire body. Lay the child, face down over the ball. Roll the ball back and forth and from side to side. Hold the child securely while rolling the ball, but allow the child to compensate for the frontward and backward and left to right movements.

5. The child can be laid on his back within a large tube and rolled from side to side making it necessary for him to compensate for any right to left movements.

6. A mattress can be used to roll a child from side to side and from stomach to back. Legs, bent at the ankles and knees as well as arms, bent at the elbows and wrists, can be moved up and down and from side to side.

Task Evaluation

1. Did the child become overtly irritated with the body manipulations?

2. Did he become frightened or tense when put into positions over the ball?

3. Did he show any compensation to movement in any direction?

4. Did he make any verbal response while being manipulated?

Materials and Equipment

Bean bag chair
Large rubber beach ball

Large hard cardboard tube
Mattress

Instructional Objective

To stimulate the body muscles and circulatory processes through the use of electric body vibrator.

Readiness

No apparent physiological impairment that would prevent or inhibit response to tactile stimulation.

Procedure

1. Lay child on soft surface, such as a carpeted floor or mattress. An electrical outlet should be close by.
2. Plug in the electric vibrator; kneel by the child.
3. Begin gently with the child so not to frighten him. Take one of his hands and rub the palm momentarily with the vibrator.
4. Hold the vibrator so the child can see it. Rub the vibrator on your face or hand, to show the child that it is safe.
5. When the child has become somewhat accustomed to the feeling on his hand, move to another area of the body.
6. Continue use of the vibrator as long as it relaxes the child, and as long as he responds favorably to it.
7. With caution, the vibrator can be used on paralyzed limbs and spastic limbs.
8. Guard against any severe tensing.

Task Evaluation

1. Did the machine seem to frighten the child? Did the noise made by the vibrator frighten him?
2. Did the child draw his limbs closer to his body when he was stimulated by the vibrator?
3. Did the child tremble or cry when stimulated by the vibrator?

4. Did child respond verbally in any way when stimulated by vibrator?

Materials and Equipment

Electric vibrator
Carpeted floor or mattress

Instructional Objective

To stimulate the body muscles and circulatory processes through the use of various brushing techniques.

Readiness

No apparent physiological impairment that would prevent or inhibit response to tactile stimulation.

Procedure

1. Lay child on soft surface such as carpeted floor or mattress.
2. Remove child's clothing from area or areas of body that you wish to stimulate.
3. Brushes to be used can range in texture from very soft to quite brisk. They can also range in size from the smallest eyeliner brush to a wallpaper brush, with many in between sizes.
4. In the first encounter of the brushing stimulation use a soft brush. This is to guard against any irritation of the child's skin. Gradually move to a harder bristle brush in later encounters.
5. Brushing should take the method of long even strokes. Be certain to be aware of any excessive skin irritation and cease the exercise in this event.
6. This stimulation can be done all over the body, but is usually begun on the hands and feet.
7. The face may be stimulated with a small eyeliner brush. At the corners of the mouth, move the brush in short swift movements up and down. (Occasionally this is done to execute a rooting and sucking reflex.) The face may also be stimulated in the area of the cheeks, eyelids and just below the lower eyelashes.

Task Evaluation

1. Did the child overtly show discontent with the brushing exercise?

2. Did any affected spastic limbs seem to relax in any way with the brushing?

3. Did the child respond verbally to the brushing?

4. Did any of the face stimulation seem to tickle him? Did he move his hand to his face or rub or scratch the itch?

Materials and Equipment

Variety of brushes (ranging in texture from very soft to hard)

Carpeted floor or mattress

Instructional Objective

To stimulate the body muscles and circulatory processes through the method of icing.

Readiness

No apparent physiological impairment that would prevent or inhibit response to tactile stimulation.

Procedure

1. This exercise can be performed on the entire body at one time, or specific areas.

2. Place the child on a soft surface lying on his back. Assure the safety of the child.

3. Remove the child's clothing from the area or areas that you wish to stimulate by the icing process.

4. Secure a large piece of ice, about three times the size of a regular ice cube.

5. Rub the desired area of the child's body in long vertical strokes.

6. Rub in intervals to stimulate but not irritate.

Task Evaluation

1. Was the child irritated with the feeling of the ice rubbing his body?
2. Did the icing cause any severe shivering of the body?

Materials and Equipment

Large piece of ice
Soft surface such as mattress

Instructional Objective

To stimulate the child's tactile senses through the use of warm and cold water.

Readiness

No apparent physiological impairment that would prevent or inhibit the response to tactile stimulation.

Procedure

1. Seat child in chair that is appropriate for his size. If the child is unable to maintain a sitting position, use a restraint such as a Posey restraint. (Fig. 7) Child's feet should be flat on the floor.
2. Secure two basins of water, one should be cold and the other quite warm.
3. Place one basin of water by the child's feet.
4. Lift his feet into the basin, and splash the water around his feet. Do this for about two minutes.
5. Then quickly move the other basin with the opposite temperature of water by his feet and submerge them in this water, splashing them.
6. This exercise can be repeated several times in one session. Make sure that there is a sharp difference in temperature.
7. This stimulation need not be confined to the feet, hands and arms. The *whole* body can be stimulated in this way. Of

Figure 7

course for the entire body stimulation, two tubs in close proximity of each other would be needed. It would be important that the child be handled easily and swiftly when taken from one tub and put into another.

8. Dry the child immediately and thoroughly when exercise is completed.

Task Evaluation

1. Did the child respond to the water exercise?
2. Did he show any evidence of being able to discriminate the

temperatures such as leaving his feet in the warm water and pulling them out of the cold water?

3. Did he respond verbally at any time?

Materials and Equipment

Two basins or two bath tubs
Warm water
Cold water
Bath towel

Instructional Objective

To stimulate the body through the use of an electric hair dryer.

Readiness

No apparent physiological impairment that would prevent or inhibit response to tactile stimulation.

Procedure

1. Lay child on soft surface such as carpeted floor or mattress. An electrical outlet should be close by.

2. Plug in the hair dryer, and then kneel by the child.

3. To reassure him that the hair dryer will not harm him, hold the hose part of it to your face or hand. The hood should not be on the end.

4. When the child has witnessed several times that the air coming from the hose will not hurt him, move the hose to his hand.

5. If the child is at all capable, encourage him to assist you in holding the hose.

6. Move the hose up and down in close proximity to his arm so that the air can be felt easily.

7. When the child becomes more relaxed with the hair dryer, move to different parts of the body.

8. Change the temperature of the hair dryer often moving

from hot to cold, so that the child may feel the difference of the two temperatures.

Task Evaluation

1. Did the machine seem to frighten the child? Did the noise made by the hair dryer frighten him?
2. Did the child make any attempt to grasp the hair dryer hose?
3. Did he seem bewildered with the source of the air?
4. Did he show any evidence of discrimination of the hot or cold air?
5. Did he make any verbal response when being stimulated by the air?

Materials and Equipment

Hair dryer (type with hose and hood)
Carpeted floor or mattress

Instructional Objective

To stimulate the child's body through a variety of tactile experiences.

Readiness

No apparent physiological impairment that would inhibit the response to tactile stimulation.

Procedure

1. This exercise is designed to stimulate the child through the use of different textures placed on the instructor's hands in contact with the child's body through manual massaging.
2. Some of the textures that the instructor can use to give a variety of feelings are: rubber gloves, silk gloves—gardening gloves, whipped cream, salt, flour paste, jelly, sandpaper, fur mittens, sand. This list can be endless with some creativity on the part of the instructor.
3. With one of the above listed textures on your hands, begin

manually massaging the child's body. When you have massaged for a length of time, change the texture on your hands to one that is quite different. An example would be to massage the child with a good bit of coarse sand on your hands, wash it off and then massage his body with cool whipped cream.

Task Evaluation

1. Did child respond to the different textures on the instructor's hands?
2. Did he show any evidence of being able to discriminate the change in texture?
3. Did he respond verbally to any of the exercising?

Materials and Equipment

Rubber gloves
Gardening gloves
Silk gloves
Whipped cream
Salt
Sand
Flour paste
Jelly
Sandpaper
Fur mittens

Instructional Objective

To stimulate the child's auditory senses.

Readiness

No apparent auditory or other physiological impairment that would prevent or inhibit response to auditory stimulation.

Procedure

1. Stimulating the child's auditory senses can be accomplished in a variety of ways. Those listed below are the beginning of a list that can be enlarged through the creativity of the instructor.

2. With a sound making device such as a decoder, or buzzer, bell, clacker (such as those used at parties) or transistor radio, go to the child and make the noise behind his head to one side or the other.

3. If at all possible, remain out of sight and keep the piece of equipment out of sight. Thus if the child responds, one can ascertain that he is responding to the sound and not to sight.

4. The sounds used should be varied often. You may want to stimulate with opposites such as a loud sharp in one ear and then a soft sound in the other.

5. Stimulation can also occur in the absence of normal background sounds. *Quiet times* as well as *sound times* serves as an important stimulation condition.

Task Evaluation

1. Did child respond to auditory stimuli in close proximity of his ear?

2. Did he seem to favor one ear over the other; thus responding more to one side?

3. Did he show in any way evidence of discrimination between auditory stimuli and the absence of it?

4. Did he respond verbally to any of the auditory stimulations?

Materials and Equipment

Decoder or buzzer
Bells
Transistor radio
Clacker

Instructional Objective

To stimulate the child's visual senses.

Readiness

No apparent visual or other physiological impairment that would prevent or inhibit response to visual stimulation.

Procedure

1. Stimulating the child visually can be accomplished in a variety of ways as in auditory stimulation. A creative instructor can add to the list below to accommodate the needs of a child.

2. Mobiles, strobe lights, twinkle lights used on Christmas trees, flashing signs such as those used in stores and flashlights are just a few of many means to stimulate visually.

3. Position the child so that he can obtain the maximum amount of stimulation from the object.

4. If using the strobe light, twinkle lights or flashing sign, the child would probably respond the best if he were seated in full view of the light.

5. When using a flashlight a game called *get the light* may provide a good bit of stimulation. If the child is nonambulatory, lay him on a mat or carpeted floor. Shine the light on his hand or another place that is easy for him to see. The object of course, is for the child to try and touch the light.

6. If a child must be left unattended, mobiles placed in the crib or playpen serve as an excellent stimulation.

7. As in the absence of sound, the absence of light can also serve as stimulation. Take the child from a brightly lighted room to a completely dark room and vice versa.

Task Evaluation

1. Did the child respond to the visual stimuli of the light games or flashing lights?

2. Did he make any attempt to play the light game?

3. Did he seem interested in the mobiles in his crib or playpen? Did he make an attempt to touch them?

4. Did he show evidence of being able to discriminate between the brightly lighted room and the dark room?

5. Did he make any verbal response to the visual stimulation?

Materials and Equipment

Mobile
Strobe light

Flashlight
Twinkle lights
Flashing sign
Multicolor rotating light

Instructional Objective

To stimulate the olfactory senses of the child.

Readiness

No apparent olfactory or other physiological impairment that would prevent or inhibit response to olfactory stimulation.

Procedure

1. Olfactory stimulation like taste stimulation is exercised through the discrimination of two distinct odors.

2. The exercise is performed to elicit any response on the part of the child to show like or dislike to a certain odor.

3. Again as with other sensory stimuli, the list of odors can be endless and should be implemented with the child in mind.

4. The child should be in the most comfortable position for him.

5. The odors should be captured in small bottles, such as those that medicine comes in.

6. With two distinct odors such as a very sweet perfume and ammonia, stimulate the child's olfactory senses by waving the small bottle directly below his nose for a period of two to three minutes, and then repeat with the other odor.

7. No more than two odors should be introduced in a single session.

Task Evaluation

1. Did the child respond to the odors?
2. Did he show any sign of discrimination of the two odors?
3. Did he respond verbally during any part of the session?

Materials and Equipment

Small bottles filled with a variety of odors such as:
Ammonia
Perfume (varied scents)
Fish
Cheese
Pine
Lemon

Instructional Objective

To stimulate the *taste* sense of the child.

Readiness

No apparent taste or other physiological impairment that would prevent or inhibit response to taste stimulation.

Procedure

1. *Taste* stimulation can be accomplished by employing a variety of tastes introduced to the child.

2. Variety of tastes can be obtained in such foods as: vinegar, lemon juice, sugar, maple syrup, salt, anchovies, liver, applesauce, ice cream. This list may be increased by a creative instructor.

3. The use of this exercise is to develop discrimination of various foods.

4. The child can either be laying or sitting during this exercise, depending upon his abilities.

5. Take two foods with very discriminate tastes such as anchovies and ice cream or lemon juice and maple syrup.

6. First give the child a taste of one food having him move it around in his mouth for two or three minutes, then give him the other.

7. No more than two different tastes should be given in one session, but a wide variety can be presented over a series of sessions.

Task Evaluation

1. Did child respond to the various tastes?
2. Did he show any evidence as to the discrimination of the two tastes?
3. Did he verbally respond during any time of the session?

Materials and Equipment

Variety of foods such as:
  Vinegar
  Lemon juice
  Sugar
  Maple syrup
  Salt
  Anchovies
  Liver
  Applesauce
  Ice cream
Spoon appropriate size for child

UNIT II
MOTOR DEVELOPMENT

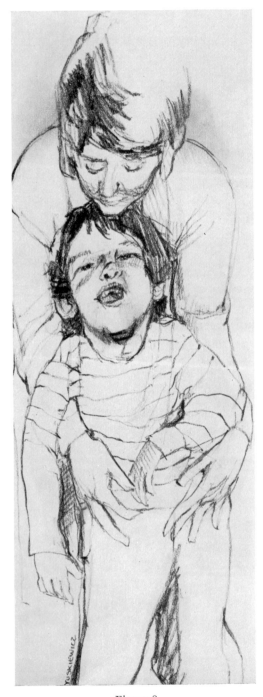

Figure 8

Competency Checklist

Name _____   Educational Facility _____

Date _____   Educator _____

Instructional Unit
Motor Development

Code:

0 No Competency

1 Moderate Competency

2 Complete Competency

. . . . 1. Moves head in the direction of sound stimulation.

. . . . 2. Lifts head while laying on abdomen.

. . . . 3. Lifts head and chest by arms when on abdomen.

. . . . 4. Reaches for objects.

. . . . 5. Sits with support.

. . . . 6. Rolls from stomach to back.

. . . . 7. Brings self to a sitting position.

. . . . 8. Stands holding on.

. . . . 9. Crawls (abdomen on floor).

. . . . 10. Creeps on hands and knees.

. . . . 11. Walks sideways holding on.

. . . . 12. Walks.

. . . . 13. Moves up steps with assistance.

. . . . Total (max. 26)

Remarks:

Instructional Objective

To have child move head in direction of sound stimulation.

Readiness

Child is able to move head voluntarily.

Child hears satisfactorily with both ears.

Procedure

1. Lay child on back on comfortable surface.
2. Child should be in such a location that it is easy to approach him from either side, e.g., a mattress or soft rug in the middle of a room.
3. The adult should kneel behind the child and make a loud noise to one side of the child's head. A bell may be used or a decoder or any other piece of equipment that makes a distinct noise that can be operated by the adult.
4. The object should not be too readily observable, making it necessary for the child to turn his head in order to locate the noise.
5. Repeat the noise making several times, going to each side of the head.
6. It is also a good idea to vary the types of sounds, such as hand clapping, music, bells, decoders and banging on drums.

Task Evaluation

1. Did the loud sounds disturb the child?
2. Did he turn his head to each side as he was stimulated by the sound?
3. Did he turn to each direction equally well?
4. Did he seem to be turning because he saw the object or because he was seeking the source of the noise?

Materials and Equipment

Mattress or soft rug for middle of floor
Bells
Decoder or buzzer
Set of small drums
Transistor radio

Instructional Objective

To have child lift head when lying on stomach.

Readiness

Child is able to remain on stomach for an extended period of time.

Child is able to control head movements: lifts head up and down.

Child balances head.

Procedure

1. Lay child on stomach on a mattress or soft rug. (Mattress or rug should be in center of room so that child is easily accessible to adult.)

2. The adult should also lie on stomach on the floor directly in front of the child. The child and adult should be face to face.

3. Encourage the child to lift his head by first giving him a small taste of pudding or similar food that he likes (Figure 9).

Figure 9

4. When he has tasted the pudding and realizes that it is on the spoon, hold it just above his head, so that it is necessary for him to lift his head to obtain the food.

5. Reward the child with another small taste of pudding when he lifts his head.

6. Gradually increase the amount of time that you require him to hold his head up before rewarding him.

Task Evaluation

1. Did the child follow the spoonful of pudding after having the first taste?

2. Would he lift his head up to try and get a second taste?

3. Did the child have to strain any to keep his head up?

Materials and Equipment

Mattress or small rug
Pudding
Spoon appropriate size for child

Instructional Objective

To have child lift head and chest by arms while on stomach.

Readiness

Child remains on stomach for an extended period of time.
Child is able to balance his head when on stomach.
Arms are strong enough and steady enough to support upper torso of body.

Procedure

1. Initially the child's body should be off floor to make it a little easier for him to lift his upper torso.

2. A wedge-type mattress is the best piece of equipment for this; however, if there is none available, a pillow placed under the child's chest may also be used.

3. Lay the child on stomach on the wedge or pillow; it should be placed to the end of the shoulders.

4. Arms should be left free and not tucked under chest.

5. Place child's hands flat on the floor, and then lift his shoulders up, thus extending his arms (Fig. 10).

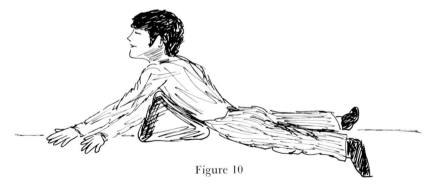

Figure 10

6. To hold attention while in this position hang a mobile in front of the child.

7. If necessary, initially support the child in this position, by holding his shoulders up, but gradually remove your support as the child becomes strong enough to support himself.

Task Evaluation

1. Did the child seem to feel comfortable lying on the wedge or pillow, or did he try to roll or squirm from the position?

2. When positioned by the adult with his hands on the floor and arms extended supporting himself, did he stay in the position or just slide or fall out of it?

3. Was he attracted to the mobile and did he raise his upper torso to look at it.

4. How long did he need the adult's assistance in maintaining the extended arm, raised upper torso position?

Materials and Equipment

Wedge like mattress or bed pillow
Mobile

Instructional Objective

To have child reach for objects.

Readiness

Child sees adequately with both eyes.
Child directs arm movements.
Child directs hand movements.
Beginning stages of grasp.

Procedure

1. Lay child on back on soft mattress or rug in an area that is accessible to the adult; it should be situated so the adult can approach the child from either side.

2. Do not elevate the head and make sure that his arms and hands are free.

3. With something that you know will attract the child's attention such as a mobile, brightly colored objects, bells or paper, go to the child and dangle it above him. This should be done approximately one foot above him within range of his hands and eyes.

4. Stimulate the child by talking to him and moving the object above him. If he doesn't begin to reach for it, move it just a little bit closer.

5. If he still doesn't attempt to reach it, take his hand and let him touch it but don't give it to him.

6. If he does begin to reach for it and does grasp it, let him have it as a reward.

7. When it is impossible for the adult to remain and hold the object, the child should be placed in a structure such as a crib or play pen with a mobile or crib gym above him.

Task Evaluation

1. Did the child seem to notice the object, and did it excite him?

2. Did he begin slapping his hands at it, but not in a grasp?

3. If he didn't initiate any movement, when you moved his hand toward it, did he resist?

4. If he did finally reach and grasp the object, was he able to maintain his grasp on it?

5. Did the crib gym or mobile interest the child?

Materials and Equipment

Brightly colored object
Crib gym
Mobile
Playtentials

Instructional Objective

To have child sit with support.

Readiness

Balances head when in a sitting position.

Has no curvature of the spine or other physical disability that would prevent the ability to be placed in a sitting position.

Procedure

1. Secure chair with solid back and side support, appropriate size for child.
2. Secure a restraint, such as a *Posey* restraint.
3. Place child in chair and then properly place restraint on him, to give optimum support while in the sitting position.
4. Position child's feet flat on the floor. If they do not comfortably reach floor, place a stool or some other piece of furniture in front of them so they will rest flatly on the surface.
5. If the child has a grasp, give him a toy to play with or some other item of interest to occupy him. If he doesn't grasp, hang a mobile or crib gym in front of him.
6. Gradually withdraw use of restraint when child has developed balance and strength to keep himself in sitting position. A chair with good arm support can be used.

Task Evaluation

1. Did child relax while in the sitting position, or did he show discomfort?
2. Was he able to hold his head erect and keep his shoulders back?
3. Would he stay in the sitting position for an extended period of time, becoming interested in the plaything?
4. Did he keep his feet positioned flat on the floor to give himself more support?

Materials and Equipment

Chair appropriate for child's size with strong back and side support

Restraint such as *Posey* restraint

Rubber toy

Mobile
Crib gym

Instructional Objective

To have child begin to roll from stomach to back.

Readiness

Directs arm movement.
Directs leg movement.
Can lift self up with arm.
Is able to roll from back to stomach.

Procedure

1. Lay child on stomach on floor covered with carpeting or blanket.
2. Place one hand flat on the floor at shoulder level. Other arm should be to child's side.
3. Assist child by holding his hand flat on the floor and giving him a small lift up and over at the shoulder to begin the rolling procedure (Fig. 11).

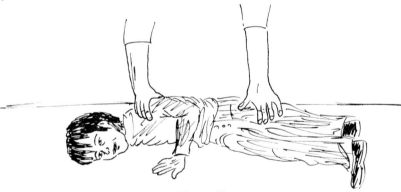

Figure 11

4. When you lift the child at the shoulder, also guide the upper leg over.

5. He should then push himself over to his back by exerting force with the hand. Instructor may assist with gentle pressure at the elbow.

Task Evaluation

1. Did the child keep his hand flat on the floor at shoulder height when it was placed there?
2. Did he extend hip and knee to help with the movement?
3. Did he exert a pushing force with his hand to make himself roll over?

Materials and Equipment

Carpeting or soft blanket

Instructional Objective

To have child bring self to a sitting position and then sit alone.

Readiness

Directs arm movements.
Directs leg movements.
Can exert a pushing force with one arm and hand.
Can balance head in a sitting position.

Procedure

1. Lay child on back on carpeted floor or on blanket placed on floor.
2. Direct child to bring arm over his body and place his hand flat on the floor at shoulder height.
3. When his hand is on the floor, direct him to bring his leg up into a bent knee position and then over to the floor on the side of the body.
4. When the child's knee is touching the floor he should exert force with the hand and arm and begin to push himself up. If

necessary, give him some assistance by a small lift at the shoulder (Fig. 12).

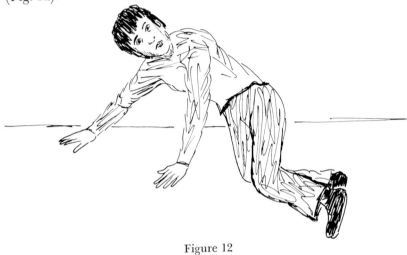

Figure 12

5. When he is approaching the sitting position, direct him to place his hand and arm on the floor and then push himself up. If necessary, help him keep his hand flat on the floor.

Task Evaluation

1. Was child able to bring arm and leg all the way over to side of body?
2. Did he keep the hand flat on the floor and push up with it?
3. Was he able to bring his arm up and place it flat on the floor to give himself support?
4. Did he need much help in bringing his upper torso up?

Materials and Equipment

Carpeted floor or blanket

Instructional Objective

To have child pull self to a standing position using support.

Readiness

Can bring self to a kneeling position.
Walks in kneeling position.
Stands with support at hips.

Procedure

1. Place a small but sturdy table in an area that is free from obstruction such as the center of a large room.

2. Place an object of interest on top of the table, such as a cookie or favorite toy.

3. Make sure that the child sees the object on the table. Encourage him to try and get the object.

4. Other than crawling over to the table, assist him by putting his hand on top of the table. (He should be in a knee-walking position.)

Figure 13

5. Direct him to push himself up to a standing position by leaning his weight on the hand placed on the table top and releasing foot from the kneeling position and placing it flat on the floor. He then should push himself up into a standing position (Fig. 13).

6. To further encourage the child to stand alone, have child hold on to your hands and momentarily let him go—slowly increasing the free standing time.

Task Evaluation

1. Did child crawl right up to the table when he saw the object?

2. Did he make an attempt to put his hand up on the table?

3. Did he bring his foot to the proper position to enable him to bring himself to a standing position?

4. Once he brought himself to a standing position did he remain standing for a length of time?

Materials and Equipment

Small sturdy table
Interesting object

Instructional Objective

To have child stand with support.

Readiness

Good grasp with both hands.
Can balance self in upright position while holding on.
Leg and back muscles developed sufficiently to hold body upright.

Procedure

1. Take child to a room with a stable piece of furniture equal to his height.

2. Make sure that nothing is on the table that might injure the child.

3. Guide him in pulling himself to a standing position using the furniture.

4. When he is at the table, position his hands and feet slightly apart to give him maximum support.

5. In order to maintain interest, place a mobile or some other item of interest nearby.

6. Length of time spent standing should be increased slightly everyday in order to build strength in legs and arms.

7. A prone board may also be used to strengthen the muscles necessary for standing (Fig. 14).

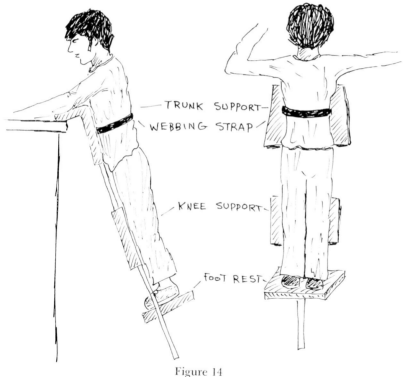

Figure 14

Task Evaluation

1. Was the child able to assume desired position?

2. If he did remain standing at table was he content to look at or play with some toy for a period of time?

3. Did he steadily increase the amount of time he was able to stand at the table?

Materials and Equipment

Piece of stable furniture equal to the height of child
Item of interest such as a mobile

Instructional Objective

To have child begin to crawl (abdomen on floor).

Readiness

Child balances head upright while on stomach.
Directs arm and hand movements.
Directs leg and foot movements.

Procedure

1. On a smooth surface such as a carpeted floor place child on stomach.

2. With a strong reinforcer such as a bowl of pudding or favorite dessert, lay down face to face in front of child.

3. Initially give him a small taste of what is in the bowl.

4. Move back so that you and the spoonful of dessert are just out of reach of the child.

5. Make sure he sees the food and then encourage him to move toward it.

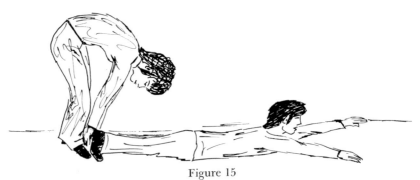

Figure 15

6. Reinforce him with a taste of the food for each attempt.

7. If he does not initiate any movement on his own, instructor should stand behind him in such a way that her feet will provide resistance to the extending leg, thus propelling the child forward. This resistance should only be offered on one leg at a time (Fig. 15).

Task Evaluation

1. Did the child equate the reinforcement (pudding) with his attempt to move forward?

2. Did he need the assistance of the instructor to move forward?

3. Did he use both his arms and legs in moving himself?

4. Did he keep his head in an upright position when moving forward?

Materials and Equipment

Carpeted floor
Appropriate reward

Instructional Objective

To have child begin to creep on hands and knees.

Readiness

Ability to crawl on abdomen.
Can hold hips off floor.

Procedure

1. Place a bed pillow on the floor.

2. Lay the child over the pillow. Place his hands and arms in such a position that he is holding his head, shoulders and chest

up. Place his knees in a kneeling position, raising hips off floor (Fig. 16).

Figure 16

3. Attract the child's attention with a mobile or some other object of interest, thus trying to build the length of time he remains in this position.

4. This exercise should be repeated until the child is able to maintain the position with ease and no longer needs the assistance of the pillow.

5. When the child can maintain the position, moving forward can be accomplished by stimulating the child to move toward something of interest such as the pudding.

6. Reward attempts of the child to move forward.

Task Evaluation

1. How long did the child need the support of the pillow?

2. When placed on the pillow, did he move his arms and legs into the appropriate position?

3. Was child's balance good when he attempted to move a leg and arm to propel himself forward?

4. Did he have a cross pattern when moving; that is right arm, left leg, alternating with left arm and right leg?

Materials and Equipment

Carpeted floor
Bed pillow
Appropriate reinforcer
Mobile

Instructional Objective

To have child begin to walk (sideways) holding on.

Readiness

Grasp.
Directs arm and leg movements.
Stands with support.
Brings self to a standing position.

Procedure

1. Take child to sofa, row of chairs or small tables.
2. Encourage the child to bring himself to a standing position either with or without support.
3. At some reasonable distance from the child, place an appropriate reward. Make sure that the child sees the reward.
4. Holding the chairs securely, encourage the child to move toward the reward.
5. If necessary, initially guide him along.
6. Gradually make the length of the chairs longer by spreading them apart, thus demanding the child *reach* for the next support.

Task Evaluation

1. Did the child crawl over to the chairs?
2. Did he seem to realize what procedure he had to go through to get the reward?
3. Did he maintain his balance in walking when a space was left between the chairs?

Materials and Equipment

Chairs
Tables
Sofas
Appropriate reward

Instructional Objective

To have the child walk with assistance.

Readiness

Pulls self to standing position.
Stands holding on.
Walks sideways.

Procedure

1. Stand behind child, take his hands in yours.

2. Gently assist him into an alternating walking pattern by (a) raising his right side by lifting his right arm, (b) throwing his entire weight onto the left leg, (c) guiding forward motion of the right side of the body with your right knee and then (d) reversal to the left side (Fig. 17).

3. When child has gained stability, release the hand and offer assistance at the shoulder.

4. Next, assist at both shoulders instead of the hands, thus demanding that the child lift his legs himself.

5. Offer him assistance only at the waist so that it is not only necessary for him to lift his legs but also balance his upper torso.

6. When he has achieved the above steps, then stand in front of him and take his hands in yours.

7. Lead him into an alternating walking pattern, by pulling on his right hand to have him move his right foot and then his left hand to move his left foot.

8. The last stage before independent walking is to encourage the child to walk into your outstretched arms.

9. Reward successful attempts at independent walking.

Task Evaluation

1. Did child follow the directional arm lead by moving appropriate foot?

2. Could child maintain stability when one hand was released?

3. Did child maintain balance of upper torso when assisted only at the waist?

4. Was child sure enough of himself to take a few independent steps into the instructor's outstretched arms?

Materials and Equipment

Open space room
Appropriate reward

Figure 17

Instructional Objective

To have child begin to move up steps with assistance.

Readiness

Child walks independently.
Maintains balance when all of his weight is on one foot.
Can shift weight from foot to foot.
Can walk up and down a ramp holding on.

Procedure

1. Take child to stairway. Direct him to hold one rail with one or both hands.
2. Instruct him to lift his one foot up and place it on the first step and then bring his other foot up to the same step.
3. When he has accomplished this have him go on until he reaches the top.
4. Do not ask child at this developmental level to descend stairs.
5. Repeat ascending stairs until child is consistently successful. Reward appropriately.

Task Evaluation

1. Was child able to lift feet high enough to reach each step?
2. Did he maintain his balance while weight was on one foot?
3. Did he hold each rail or did he hold one rail with both hands?

Materials and Equipment

Stairway or training steps
Appropriate reward

Specific Motor Activities for the Spastic and Athetoid Child
by
Uta Dreher
Registered Physical Therapist

The following supplementary tasks have been designed for teacher use to prepare the spastic and athetoid child for the motor development program. The objectives are to provide a means for the spastic child to experience movement and the athetoid child to discover posture.

Instructional Objective

To bring the athetoid cerebral palsied child to a more stabilized posture.

Readiness

No apparent physiological impairment that would prevent or inhibit the development of stabilized posture.
Can lay on stomach for moderate period of time.

Procedure

1. The stabilization procedure should start by laying the athetoid child on his stomach on a flat surface such as a carpeted floor.

2. The object of the exercise is for the child to maintain straight alignment and a stable body position for a length of time.

3. When the child can remain laying calm face down on the floor without falling to one side or the other, introduce the next step.

4. This step is for the athetoid to hold his head erect while laying on his stomach. He should be resting the weight of his upper torso on his elbows.

5. To develop the length of time that the child is able to re-

main calm and hold his position, catch his interest in a mobile, a story told to him by an adult or a television program.

Task Evaluation

1. Did child fall to one side when placed stomach down on floor?
2. Were child's arms strong enough to support the weight of his upper torso?
3. By following the procedure, was it apparent that the child remained in one position for a longer period of time?

Materials and Equipment

Soft surface such as carpeted floor
Mobile
Story book
Television

Instructional Objective

To have the athetoid cerebral palsied child maintain a side sitting position.

Readiness

Can maintain a sitting position without support.
Can hold body weight on outstretched arms.

Procedure

1. Lay child face down on soft flat surface.
2. Roll child to right side so that he is supporting himself on his right elbow and straight left arm.
3. Stabilize his left hand on the floor and begin to bring child up by assisting him with a pull on the right shoulder. When he is about halfway up, bend his knees and hips, then help him push his upper torso into the complete sitting position.
4. His weight is resting on his hands and right hip.

5. This exercise should also be done to the left side of the body.

6. This therapeutic posture is useful and beneficial for any activities normally done on the floor, such as eye tracking, focusing, stimulating head control and storytime exercises.

7. A further developmental stage of this procedure is for the child to gain the competency to maintain the side sitting posture without the support of his hands.

8. If the child is side sitting to the right he will need the support of his right hand longer than the left hand. The goal is to have the child side sit without the support of either hand and accomplish movement in any given direction on command.

Task Evaluation

1. Did the child become overly excited and fall to one side as soon as he was positioned on his stomach?

2. Did he favor one side by leaning to that side?

3. Were his arms strong enough and stable enough to hold his upper torso erect?

4. Was the child able to approximate side sitting without support of hands?

Materials and Equipment

Soft surface such as a carpeted floor
Mobile
Book
Television

Instructional Objective

To develop a relaxed state in the spastic child.

Readiness

No apparent physiological impairment that would prevent or inhibit the development of a relaxed state.

Can lay on side for a moderate period of time.

Procedure

1. Instructor should be in back of child.

2. Child should be laying on the convex (usually the side with the rib hump), head at the right of the instructor.

3. Place heel of your hand that is closest to child's head on his rib cage.

4. Fingers of hand closest to child's hip should be on the upper crest of the child's pelvic bone (Fig. 18).

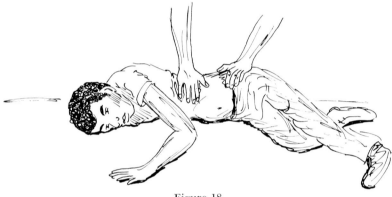

Figure 18

5. At the same time, push forward with hand on rib cage while pulling backward with fingers of hand on pelvic bone.

6. Reverse the procedure. The hand that pushes forward now pulls backward and vice versa. The motion should be similar to kneading.

7. Each sequence should take approximately, or at least, two seconds.

8. When you see that the child's spastic arm and leg become more relaxed, place a small pillow between the child's knee (so that knee is at same level with hip).

9. Use child's arm on floor side as a pillow for his head.

10. To achieve relaxation, this procedure may take up to ten minutes in the beginning and approximately two minutes when the child becomes used to the exercise.

11. Make note that as soon as you make an abrupt motion, the

child will return to his spasticity. It is necessary to guard against this.

Task Evaluation

1. Did child become disturbed by being exercised in this manner?
2. Did the spastic limbs show any sign of relaxation through the implementation of the procedure?
3. Did child respond verbally or in an other way to the exercise?

Materials and Equipment

Soft surface such as carpeted floor or mat

Instructional Objective

To relax spasticity and extend limbs of the child.

Readiness

No apparent physiological impairment that would prevent or inhibit the extension of limbs.

Procedure

1. Secure beach ball large enough to accommodate child's entire body.
2. Place child on stomach over ball.
3. To make him feel comfortable, reassure him with the pressure of your hands and body holding him firmly.
4. Rock and bounce him gently.
5. Continue until the child relaxes and you notice the spasticity reduce by the extension of the limbs.
6. The bouncing releases the grip of the spasticity so that gravity pulls the limbs into extension and limply rest on the ball.
7. This readies the spastic child for voluntary activities.

Task Evaluation

1. Did child become disturbed when placed over ball?
2. Did he become reassured by the instructor's firm hold?
3. Did the child gradually extend his limbs?
4. Did child remain relaxed for a period of time after being taken off the ball?

Materials and Equipment

Beach ball large enough to accommodate entire body

Instructional Objective

To develop head control in the spastic and athetoid child.

Readiness

Lifts head when in a prone position.
Turns head from side-to-side in a prone position.
Attempts to sit.

Procedure

1. Sit child on your lap. His legs should be spread over your hips such as sitting on a horse.
2. If child does not hold his head in a position of straight alignment, do it for him.
3. Gently upset the balance of the child's head, first by tilting trunk slightly to one side and then the other. If the head flops, you have tilted him too much and the action should be minimized.
4. The tilting should also be done forward and backward.
5. This procedure should be repeated often. It applies for any lack of head control, spastics, athetoids and floppy children.

Task Evaluation

1. Did child become disturbed with this exercise?

2. If it was necessary to position child's head in straight alignment, did he keep it that way?

3. Did child lose balance when moved to right, left, forward or backward?

Materials and Equipment

Soft surface such as carpeted floor or mat

UNIT III
SELF-CARE DEVELOPMENT

Figure 19

Competency Checklist

Name _____   Educational Facility _____

Date _____   Educator _____

Instructional Unit
Self-Care Development
(Self Feeding and Drinking)

Code:
0 No Competency
1 Moderate Competency
2 Complete Competency

.... 1. Takes fluids from a dropper.
.... 2. Sucks.
.... 3. Swallows.
.... 4. Bottle feeds.
.... 5. Eats pureed food from a spoon in a reclining position.
.... 6. Eats pureed food from a spoon in a sitting position.
.... 7. Takes liquids from a trainer cup with a sucking spout.
.... 8. Takes liquids from a glass with a straw attached.
.... 9. Chews.
.... 10. Eats chopped regular food from a spoon in a reclining position.
.... 11. Eats chopped regular food from a spoon while maintaining a sitting position.
.... 12. Finger feeds.
.... 13. Uses a hand over hand method, with the help of the instructor, in feeding himself.
.... 14. In a hand over hand method drinks from a small cup.
.... 15. Spoon feeds himself scooping the food from a bowl.

.... 16. Spoon feeds himself with spoon from a plate
with a guard for assistance.
.... 17. Holds and drinks from a cup.
.... 18. Eats bite size pieces of food using a fork.
.... 19. Drinks from a glass held by himself.
.... 20. Can manipulate a knife and fork.
.... Total (max. 40)
Remarks:

Instructional Objective

To teach child to take nourishment through dropper feeding.

Readiness

Esophagus open so that liquids and strained cereals may pass easily.

Procedure

1. Lay child on back.
2. With thumb on child's cheek and index finger on chin, open his mouth.

Task Evaluation

1. Did child gag when food was placed on his tongue?

Materials and Equipment

Food dropper
Suggested food:
  Milk
  Vitamin supplement
  Cereal

Instructional Objective

To teach child sucking process.

Readiness

Esophagus opened sufficiently to permit small amounts of liquids and strained foods to pass easily.

Procedure

1. With dropper, place moderate amount of apple cider vinegar on child's tongue. Check sensitivity of tongue such as the tip. This may also be done with lemon juice. The vinegar or lemon juice should be placed on the front part of the tongue, rather than the back.

2. This procedure should be followed until the child automatically sucks as soon as a drop of any liquid is placed on the tongue.

Task Evaluation

1. Does child's tongue go up to the roof of his mouth or make any sucking action when lemon juice or vinegar is placed on it?

Materials and Equipment

Food dropper
Lemon juice
Apple cider vinegar

Instructional Objective

To teach child to swallow.

Readiness

Esophagus opened sufficiently to permit passage of food.

Procedure

1. Place child in a reclining position.
2. Instructor's hand should be in the following position: middle finger under the child's chin at the root of the tongue. This controls the tongue movement. The index finger is on the chin directly under the lower lip. This will control up and down movement. The thumb on the cheek (Fig. 20).

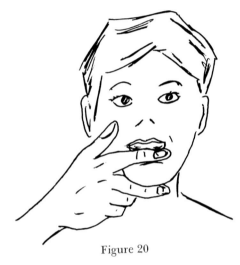

Figure 20

3. Place food on the middle of the tongue.
4. With index finger and thumb close child's mouth.
5. Firmly hold the root of the tongue. This prohibits a forward movement and encourages the child to swallow and get air.

Task Evaluation

1. Did child resist the instructor's hand on his face?
2. Did child try to force food from mouth even though tongue movements were being controlled?

Materials and Equipment

Slightly pureed food such as:
   Junior foods
   Mashed potatoes

Instructional Objective

To teach child to bottle feed.

Readiness

Child has developed sucking reflex.
Child is able to swallow liquids.

Procedure

1. Introduce bottle into child's mouth.
2. Stimulate the tongue by moving the bottle nipple from side to side. This will help to get some milk from the bottle and to motivate the child to suck.
3. Initially the opening in the nipple should be large enough so that the child does not have to suck vigorously. However, the opening shouldn't be so large that the milk flows too fast for the child to swallow easily.

Task Evaluation

1. Did nipple just sit in child's mouth, or did he suck on it?
2. Was child able to swallow the flow of milk easily?

Materials and Equipment

Baby bottle
Milk
Juice

Instructional Objective

To teach child to eat pureed food from a spoon while in a reclining position.

Readiness

Ability to suck and swallow.

Procedure

1. Lay child in a reclining position.
2. Elevate head.
3. Place small amount of the food on the back of the tongue.
4. Instructor's middle finger should be under the child's chin at the root of his tongue, thus to control tongue movement (Fig. 21).

Figure 21

5. The instructor's index finger should be on the chin directly under the lower lip and the thumb on his cheek. This enables the instructor to control opening and closing of the mouth and tongue movement as described in step 4.

6. By controlling the tongue the child can't bring his tongue out of his mouth. By having his lips held shut, he is forced to swallow to get a breath.

Task Evaluation

1. Did the food just drain down the throat or did the tongue move to direct the food?

2. Did the child resist the guided movements of the instructor?

3. Was there a foreward tongue movement pushing the food toward the lips rather than toward the esophagus?

Materials and Equipment

Pillow for head
Strained baby food
Pureed food (the texture of baby food)

Instructional Objective

To teach child to eat pureed food while in a sitting position.

Readiness

Child's esophagus is open sufficiently to pass pureed food.
Child is able to swallow in an upright position.

Procedure

1. Initially prop up child with pillow into a half sitting half reclining position.

2. Place food on the back of the tongue with spoon.

3. If the child doesn't close his lips, close them for him.

4. If he moves his tongue forward instead of to each side, hold the root of the tongue under the chin.

5. Gradually move the child into a sitting position, having as a goal his sitting on a chair at a table.

6. Gradually move the food forward on the tongue, with a spoon, encouraging the child to manipulate the food from a sitting position.

Task Evaluation

1. While in a sitting position, did child keep the food in his mouth or did it drip out?

2. Did child just keep the food in his mouth and not swallow?

3. Did child suck the food down rather than swallow?

Materials and Equipment

Pureed foods
Soft foods such as melted ice cream
Pudding
Mashed potatoes
Squash

Instructional Objective

To have child drink from a trainer cup with a sucking spout.

Readiness

Ability to swallow liquids in a constant flow.
Sucking response present.

Procedure

1. Introduce cup to child. Ask him if he wants a drink.
2. Place child's hands around the cup or through the handle if there is one on the cup.
3. Place sucking spout into his mouth. If he doesn't begin to suck, push his cheeks in and out until he begins to suck.

Task Evaluation

1. Did spout just lay in mouth or did child suck from it?
2. Was child able to swallow the liquid as fast as it came from the spout?

Materials and Equipment

Trainer cup with handle and sucking spout

Instructional Objective

To have child drink from a straw.

Readiness

Child balances head.

Child is able to maintain a sitting position and can compensate for any move to the right or left.

Child is able to suck.

Procedure

1. Seat child at table that enables the instructor to sit opposite him.

2. Introduce the plastic glass with straw to the child.

3. Encourage him to place one hand around the straw and the other hand around the glass.

4. If child does not direct his own mouth to the straw, aid him.

5. Instructor should manipulate his cheeks in and out if he does not begin to suck showing him that when he does suck, he can make the top of the glass spin around (Fig. 22).

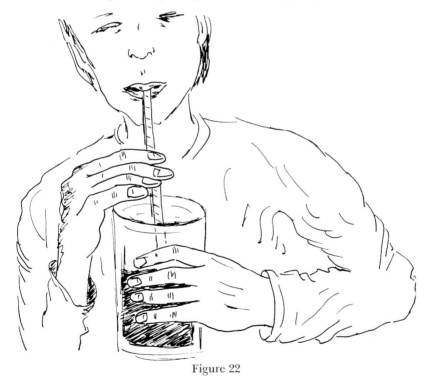

Figure 22

Task Evaluation

1. Did the child suck and swallow the liquid or did most of the liquid run out of his mouth before he could swallow it?

2. Did the child hold the glass in place or did it slide over the table?

Materials and Equipment

Sip 'n Spin plastic glass with top and straw coming out of side of glass

Instructional Objective

To teach child chewing process.

Readiness

Ability to swallow.
Will accept a textured food in the mouth.

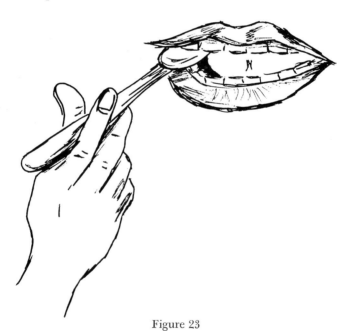

Figure 23

Procedure

1. Sit child in a position to the side of the instructor so that it is easy to guide mouth movements. Place arm around head and position hand in the same manner as explained earlier with spoon feeding. That is middle finger at root of tongue, index finger on chin and thumb on cheek.

2. Introduce a small amount of food to one side of the child's mouth, between the teeth (Fig. 23).

3. If the child does not close his mouth, gently manipulate index finger and thumb to close it. Hold middle finger firmly under chin at root of tongue to prohibit tongue from pushing food out of mouth.

4. Gently manipulate index finger and thumb to move child's jaws up and down (Fig. 24).

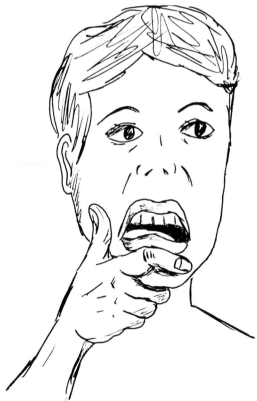

Figure 24

5. If food moves to center of mouth with the spoon, move back to one side between the teeth.

Task Evaluation

1. Was there initial jaw movement when food was placed between the teeth?
2. Did the tongue move from the center to side rather than forward?

Materials and Equipment

Chopped food such as noodles or some other food that is chewable that if not chewed sufficiently should not be difficult to swallow

Instructional Objective

To teach child alternate chewing process.

Readiness

Ability to swallow.
Will accept foreign object in mouth.

Procedure

1. Sit child in such a position that it is very easy for instructor to manipulate jaw movement.
2. Secure a long narrow piece of sirloin steak approximately 4 inches long by $3/4$ inch wide.
3. Put one end of the steak in child's mouth to one side and between his teeth. The other end of the steak should be in the hand of the instructor (Fig. 25).
4. The instructor should place his hand in such a way that he can manipulate the child's jaws in an up and down movement and at the same time hold one end of the steak.

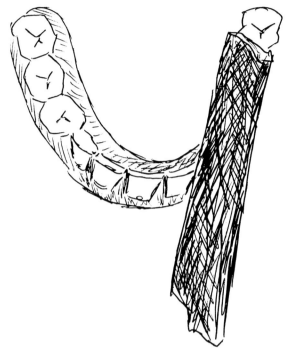

Figure 25

Task Evaluation

1. Did child choke or gag when the steak was placed in his mouth?

2. Did child move his mouth up and down in a chewing motion or did he just let the steak lay to the side of his mouth?

Materials and Equipment

Raw sirloin steak, 4 inches long, ¾ inch wide

Instructional Objective

To have child successfully chew and swallow chopped food in a reclining position.

Readiness

Esophagus open sufficiently to pass solids.
Child has ability to swallow.
Chewing motion is present.

Procedure

1. Place child in reclining position with head propped on pillow.
2. Introduce the food to him telling him just what it is he is going to eat.
3. Place food just on the tip of the spoon and encourage the child to use his lips to take the food off the spoon, rather than having the instructor slide the food from the spoon (Fig. 26).

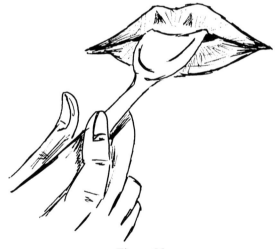

Figure 26

4. Throughout the feeding encourage the child to take the food with his lips.
5. If he needs help chewing and if the food just lays in his mouth after he has taken it from the spoon, use the spoon to place the food between his teeth to one side of the mouth and manipulate his jaws until he responds.

Task Evaluation

1. Did child use his lips to take the food from the spoon?
2. Did the food just lay in the child's mouth or did he push it to one side with his tongue?

Materials and Equipment

Chopped food such as meatloaf, green beans, carrots, peas
Noodles
This food should be large enough that it has to be chewed a few times before it is swallowed, but not quite bite size.

Instructional Objective

To have child sufficiently chew and swallow chopped table food while in a sitting position.

Readiness

Child is able to chew.
Child is able to swallow solids as well as liquids.
Child balances head.
Child maintains a sitting position.

Procedure

1. Sit child at a table that enables the instructor to sit opposite.
2. Introduce the child to the food he is going to eat.
3. Put some food on the end of a spoon and place to the child's mouth. Encourage him to take the food from the spoon with his lips.
4. Notice the child's tongue movements. If they are forward and backward rather than to the side, hold his lips together so that he is unable to move his tongue forward. Thus, he will be unable to push the food from his mouth.
5. Do not permit the child to place the tongue out of the

mouth when taking the food. Touch his tongue with your finger until he keeps it in. Then introduce the food.

Task Evaluation

1. Did child take the food with his lips?
2. Did child move his tongue forward, backward or push the food out?

Materials and Equipment

Table that enables child and instructor to sit opposite each other

Chopped table food large enough to require chewing but not quite bite size including meatloaf, peas, green beans, carrots and noodles

Instructional Objective

To have child finger feed chopped regular food.

Readiness

Balances head.

Remains in a sitting position.

Is able to chew.

Swallows sufficiently while in a sitting position.

Pincer movement developed to point that child can pick up food with three or four fingers.

Procedure

1. Sit child at table and make comfortable before introducing food.
2. Instructor should sit opposite child and guide movements.
3. Introduce two or three pieces of bite size food.
4. If child does not begin to pick up food, the instructor should place one of the pieces in the child's hand and guide the hand to the mouth (Fig. 27).

Figure 27

5. Step four should be repeated if child does not begin to pick at or play with food first.

6. If child does begin to pick at food, wait until he has a piece of food in his hand and then guide the hand to his mouth.

Task Evaluation

1. Did child sustain interest in finger feeding?
2. Did child learn that the food was to go into his mouth?
3. Was pincer grasp developed to the point of delivering the food from the table to the mouth without dropping it several times?
4. Did child eat the food or play with it?

Materials and Equipment

Table which enables instructor to sit opposite child

Bite size pieces of food, such as french fries or pieces of meatloaf

Instructional Objective

To have child successfully develop a hand over hand method of feeding.

Readiness

Balances head.

Has grasp.

Remains in a sitting position.

Procedure

1. Instructor sit to side of child.
2. Instructor's hand should be over child's hand, thus enabling him to hold spoon. This is the hand over hand method.
3. Instructor's other hand should be supporting the elbow of the child's arm (Fig. 28).

Figure 28

4. With the assistance of the instructor, the child should scoop food from the bowl and place in mouth.
5. The instructor should then guide the child's arm and hand back to the bowl.
6. Reward the child each time he goes through this procedure successfully. Remember to hold child's hand and elbow firmly so

that he senses the support, but not so tightly as to discourage his initiative.

Task Evaluation

1. Did child offer resistance to hand and elbow support?
2. Did child take initiative in directing spoon toward the mouth?

Materials and Equipment

Large handled spoon

Mashed potatoes along with a chopped meat or vegetable to help keep the food on the spoon to enable the child to be more successful in the task of getting the food from the bowl to his mouth without having it fall from the spoon

Instructional Objective

To have child hold a small cup with the hand over hand assistance of the instructor.

Readiness

Child balances head.

Child can maintain a sitting position and maintain movement.

Child has developed the beginnings of a grasp.

Procedure

1. Sit child at table that enables instructor to sit to his side.
2. Place both hands of the child around a cup. Instructor's hand should be over the child's.
3. Help child raise the cup to his mouth.
4. If the child has difficulty in keeping the liquid in his mouth, position cup to roof of his mouth. This will enable him to take the liquid from the cup more easily.
5. Gradually move the cup into a normal drinking position and withdraw assistance.

Task Evaluation

1. Did the child have difficulty in getting the liquid from the cup?
2. Did most of the liquid drain from the child's mouth before he was able to swallow it?
3. Did the liquid flow too fast for the child to easily swallow it?

Materials and Equipment

Plastic cup appropriate to the size of the child's hand

Instructional Objective

To have child successfully feed himself from a bowl using a spoon.

Readiness

Has good balance and can compensate for movement to left and right.
Has grasp.
Can use a spoon.

Procedure

1. Place child at a table which enables instructor to sit opposite.
2. Place bowl of food in front of child and hand him a spoon. If necessary, use therapy spoon with large handle (Fig. 29).
3. For the first two or three spoonfuls, go through the motions

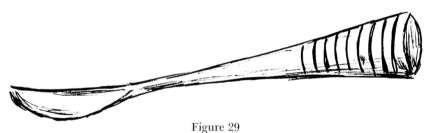

Figure 29

of scooping the food for him. Verbalize to the child while going through the procedure.

4. Encourage the child after you have demonstrated the task to continue the procedure on his own.

Task Evaluation

1. Did child push food out of his mouth with tongue movements?

2. Did child scoop food and feed himself?

Materials and Equipment

Therapy spoon

Instructional Objective

To have child successfully spoon feed himself from a plate, with a plate guard attached.

Readiness

Child balances himself in a sitting position.

Can direct arm and hand movements well enough to scoop from plate.

Procedure

1. Sit child at table.

2. Place plate of food on table in manner so that the metal plate guard is away from child (Fig. 30).

Figure 30

3. Demonstrate spoon feeding by going through the motions of scooping the food with the spoon by pushing the food against the guard (Fig. 31).

Figure 31

4. After allowing the child to go through the procedure several times encourage him to place spoon under the food.

Task Evaluation

1. Did child push the plate while pushing the food toward the plate guard?
2. Did the child become successful in scooping the food?

Materials and Equipment

Plate guard
Table that enables instructor to sit opposite child
Foods that are easy to scoop such as mashed potatoes and baked
   beans

Instructional Objective

To have child hold and drink from cup independently.

Readiness

Child balances head.
Child maintains a sitting position.
Grasp is developed.

Procedure

1. Sit child at table that enables instructor to sit opposite him.
2. Introduce the cup of liquid to the child.
3. Hold it until child grasps it. Assist if necessary.
4. After he has directed the cup to his mouth and taken a drink, help direct his arm back to the table to place the cup.

Task Evaluation

1. Did the child tip the cup before he got it to his mouth?
2. Was child able to drink and return cup to the table?

Materials and Equipment

Cup correct size for child to manage
Liquid enjoyed by child

Instructional Objective

To have child successfully feed himself bite size food from a plate using a fork.

Readiness

Child has good balance and can compensate for any right or left movement.

Grasp is developed sufficiently to hold fork.

Procedure

1. Sit child at table.
2. Place bite size pieces of food on plate in front of child.
3. Hand child fork and place his other hand on edge of plate. Direct him in the required piercing motion (Fig. 32).
4. Repeat several times until child realizes that he must touch the food with the fork and press down.
5. Verbalize each procedural step to the child concurrent with the action.

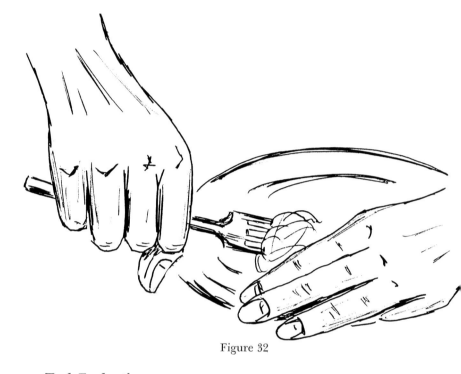

Figure 32

Task Evaluation

1. Did child have strength to pierce food?
2. Did child realize he could prevent plate from slipping by piercing with one hand and holding the plate with the other?
3. Was the child successful in performing the task?

Materials and Equipment

Fork appropriate to the size of the child's hand
Food easy to pierce and pick up with a fork, such as cut up hot dog

Instructional Objective

To have child hold and drink from glass independently.

Readiness

Child balances head and maintains a sitting position.
Grasp is present.
Good control of grasp and hand movements.

Procedure

1. Sit child at table appropriate for his size.
2. Introduce the glass of liquid to the child.
3. Demonstrate to the child that he should put his four fingers on one side of the glass and his thumb on the other and grip firmly.

Task Evaluation

1. Did the child tip the glass and spill the liquid?
2. Was the child able to grip the glass without the aid of a handle as on a cup?

Materials and Equipment

Glass (plastic suggested) appropriate to size of child's hand
Liquid enjoyed by child

Instructional Objective

To have child successfully cut food using a knife.

Readiness

Child is able to take food from a plate.
Child successfully feeds himself using a fork.

Procedure

1. Place child at a table that enables instructor to sit opposite.
2. Introduce the food on the plate.
3. Hand the child a knife. It should be held with one hand and the fork in the other.

4. With a hand over hand method, demonstrate to the child the manner in which he should pierce the food with the fork and hold the knife in the other hand.

5. After the child has demonstraetd the ability to pierce food, show the child, using the hand over hand method, how he can push forward and pull backward on the knife, using a steady motion, to cut the food (Fig. 33).

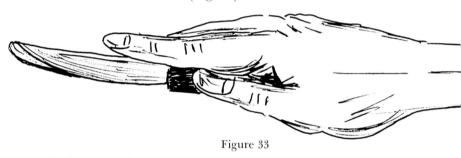

Figure 33

Task Evaluation

1. Was child able to hold fork with one hand and knife in the other?

2. Did the child tear at food with knife or were his motions steady?

Materials and Equipment

Knife appropriate to size of child's hand
Foods that are easy to cut such as pancakes or meatloaf

Competency Checklist

Name _____   Educational Facility_____

Date _____   Educator_____

**Instructional Unit
Self Care Development
(Washing and Bathing)**

Code:

  0 No Competency
  1 Moderate Competency
  2 Complete Competency

.... 1. Child remains in bathtub for an extended period of time.

.... 2. Plays in bathroom sink by keeping hands under running faucet.

.... 3. Attempts to wash self with a washcloth.

.... 4. Tries to apply soap to the washcloth.

.... 5. Washes all parts of his body except face.

.... 6. Dries self with assistance.

.... 7. Helps adult wash and dry his face.

.... 8. Washes and dries hands and face independently.

.... Total (max. 16)

Remarks:

Instructional Objective

To have child relax in bathtub of water.

Readiness

Child has good head balance.
Child sits without support.
Child has grasp.
Child is not afraid of water.

Procedure

1. Fill tub with lukewarm water to cover child's legs when sitting.

2. The bathtub should have the water in it before child is put in.

3. Assist the child in getting into the bathtub and help him to sit down. A bath mat may be of assistance and prevent slipping. Insist that the child remain sitting when he is in the tub.

4. Introduce a few rubber toys and a wash cloth.

5. Using a hand over hand method help the child wash the toys.

6. The object is to have the child accept sitting in the bathtub of water long enough to thoroughly clean himself. Also we want the child to begin to realize that by rubbing the wash cloth over dirt he can remove it.

Task Evaluation

1. Was child satisfied to stay in the tub of water for an extended period of time?
2. Did he try to stand up while in the tub?
3. Did he get the idea of using the washcloth to clean off dirt?

Materials and Equipment

Fully equipped bathroom
Rubber toys such as ducks and dolls
Lukewarm water
Bath mat

Instructional Objective

To have child put hands under running faucet in sink.

Readiness

Child stands alone or with the support of a sink.
Child is not frightened by running water.

Procedure

1. Take the child to the bathroom and have him stand in front of the sink. If he is too short to comfortably put his hands under the running water, a small set of steps or a step stool should be placed in front of the sink for the child to stand on.
2. Turn the water on making it lukewarm in temperature.
3. Give the child the command, (name), wash your hands!
4. If the child does not readily put his hands under the running water, guide them for him gently without force.
5. When he has his hands under the water, move them over each other in a washing motion.

Task Evaluation

1. Did the child seem afraid of getting his hands wet?
2. Did child cooperate in standing at the sink?
3. Could he maintain his balance while moving his hands under water?

Materials and Equipment

Bathroom sink
Small set of steps or step stool
Lukewarm water

Instructional Objective

To have child attempt to wash body with washcloth while in bathtub or hands at sink.

Readiness

Child has good head balance.
Child sits without support.
Child has grasp.
Child stands at sink by himself or with grasp support.

Procedure

1. Fill bathtub with water to cover child's legs while sitting or fill bathroom sink about one-third way full. The water should be lukewarm.
2. Attract child's attention by saying, (name), let's take a bath!
3. Assist child into bathtub and command him to sit down. Bath mat is recommended to prevent slipping.
4. Hand child the washcloth and in a hand over hand method assist him in washing himself.
5. The communication during this period should be as follows: (name), wash your arm! Follow through, (name), wash

your stomach! Follow through and continue to other parts of the body.

6. Go over the child's entire body by naming the parts before helping him wash.

7. Again, when the child is at the sink, give him the command (name), wash your hands!

Task Evaluation

1. Did child maintain good grasp on washcloth?
2. Did child resist having washcloth cross any body parts?
3. Did he begin to follow commands after naming parts of the body several times?

Materials and Equipment

Fully equipped bathroom with tub and sink
Washcloth
Bath mat
Lukewarm water

Instructional Objective

To have child apply soap to washcloth and wash body.

Readiness

Child has strong grasp.
Can grasp with both hands.
Coordinates hand movement.

Procedure

1. Fill bathtub or sink partially.
2. Assist child into tub or to sink.
3. Hand the soap to the child. He should be able to hold it.
4. Hand child a washcloth in his other hand.
5. Using a hand over hand method have the child rub the soap on the washcloth.
6. If necessary, give the hand holding the washcloth support.

7. When child has a sufficient amount of soap on the wash-cloth, he should be instructed to put the soap in the soap dish and transfer washcloth to his hand of preference. Command him to wash certain parts of his body, i.e., (name), wash your leg!

8. If necessary, guide his hand to the leg and help him rub the cloth and soap over it.

9. Demonstrate to him using a hand over hand method that he can get the soap from the washcloth by moving it back and forth in the water and squeezing it to get most of the water from it.

10. When the cloth is free of the soap, he should rub it over the part of the body that was washed in order to rinse it.

11. Repeat steps 3 through 10 until child is consistently successful.

Task Evaluation

1. Did child hold soap tightly enough to apply soap to the washcloth without it slipping out of his hand?

2. Was he able to hold the washcloth securely in his hand long enough to put the soap on it?

3. Was he able to put the soap in the soap dish and transfer the washcloth to other hand without great difficulty?

4. Was he capable of rinsing the soap from the washcloth and rinsing himself?

Materials and Equipment

Fully equipped bathroom
Bath mat
Washcloth
Soap
Soap dish
Lukewarm water

Instructional Objective

To have child wash independently except for face.

Readiness

Child sits in bathtub without support.
Will stay in tub for extended period of time.
Has good strong grasp.
Can alternate functions between hands.

Procedure

1. Guide child into a partially filled tub. Water should be warm.
2. Command the child to sit down. Assist if necessary.
3. Hand child the soap.
4. While he is holding the soap, hand him a wash cloth.
5. Give him the command, (name), put some soap on the wash-cloth! Aid him only if he does not initiate the activity.
6. When he has soap on the washcloth, give him the command, (name), wash your stomach (other part of body)! Assist only if he does not initiate the activity on his own.
7. Instruct him to rinse his body by removing the soap from the washcloth and going over the soapy body parts.
8. He should be permitted to wash and rinse his entire body in this manner. Let him be as independent as possible.
9. He may neglect his face. This could be related to fear of getting soap in his eyes. He should not be forced; instead, wash his face for him gently.

Task Evaluation

1. Did child seem to have good control when applying soap to the washcloth?
2. Did he follow immediately when given the command to wash certain parts of his body or did he need assistance?
3. Did he rinse the soap from the washcloth adequately before rinsing himself?

Materials and Equipment

Fully equipped bathroom
Bath mat

Washcloth
Soap
Soap dish
Lukewarm water

Instructional Objective

To have child dry himself with assistance.

Readiness

Grasp with both hands.
Can use both hands in a simultaneous rubbing motion.

Procedure

1. Assist child out of bathtub.
2. Direct child to stand on a rug or towel to avoid slipping. If unable to stand, seat him on towel or rug.
3. Hand child the towel. It should not be a regular bath size towel, but one a size smaller. The large size is usually cumbersome to handle.
4. Instruct the child to grasp the towel with both hands.
5. Give him the command, (name), dry your stomach, etc.!
6. If necessary, guide his hands by using hand over hand and assist him in drying each part of his body.
7. Explain as you go along that both hands should be used in a rubbing up and down motion. When drying each arm, the opposite hand will be used.

Task Evaluation

1. Did child maintain good grasp on towel?
2. Was he able to hold it while drying the body?
3. How much assistance did he require?

Materials and Equipment

Towel—one size smaller than usual
Rug or large towel for sitting or standing on

Instructional Objective

To have child wash and dry face with assistance.

Readiness

Child has accepted soap and water on his face.
Child has grasp.
Child can put soap on washcloth and rinse.

Procedure

1. Place child in tub of lukewarm water and let him wash himself except for his face.

2. When he has completed the task, ask him to put some soap on a washcloth.

3. When he has done this, give him the command, (name), wash your face!

4. Direct his hands with the washcloth over his face.

5. In a hand over hand method guide him in washing his face, being careful to avoid his eyes.

6. When his face is clean, direct him to rinse the washcloth.

7. Again, in a hand over hand manner, help him rinse the soap from his face.

8. To have the child help to dry his face, use the same method as described in step four with the washcloth. Place the towel over his hands and guide them to his face. Have him move the towel up and down over his face to dry the water from it.

Task Evaluation

1. Did child appear to be afraid to put the soapy washcloth on his face?

2. Did child tap at his face with the washcloth or did he use strong up and down motions to clean his face?

3. Did child adequately dry his face or did he just touch it with the towel rather than using an up and down sweeping motion to dry it?

Materials and Equipment

Fully equipped bathroom
Soap

Bath mat
Washcloth
Towel—one size smaller than bath
Lukewarm water

Instructional Objective

To have child wash and dry entire body independently.

Readiness

Grasps.
Accepts soap and water on entire body.
Can use washcloth on entire body.
Uses towel in drying entire body.

Procedure

1. Fill bathtub partially with lukewarm water.
2. Aid child in getting into bathtub.
3. Command child to sit down.
4. When child is sitting, give the command, (name), wash your arm, etc.!
5. If he does not begin to pick up the soap and washcloth, encourage him by handing him the washcloth and soap.
6. Again, give him the command, (name), wash your arm!
7. When he has washed his arm completely, command him to rinse his arm. Follow same procedure until he has washed his entire body.
8. When he has completely finished washing, command him to step out of the tub.
9. Show child where the towel is hanging, but do not get it for him. Give him the command, (name), get the towel!
10. When he has the towel, give him the command, (name), dry your arm! If he does not initiate the activity, guide his hand to start. Let him continue to dry his own body.
11. When he has finished drying himself, command him to hang the towel on the rack.

Task Evaluation

1. Did child apply the soap to the washcloth and wash himself when given the command?
2. Did he have trouble washing any parts of his body such as his back or neck?
3. Did he rinse the soap from his body completely?
4. Was he able to get the towel from the towel rack?
5. Did he dry himself adequately or did he experience difficulty?
6. Was he able to return the towel to the rack?

Materials and Equipment

Fully equipped bathroom
Bath mat
Wash cloth
Towel—one size smaller than usual
Soap
Lukewarm water

Competency Checklist

Name_____   Educational Facility_____

Date_____   Educator_____

Instructional Unit
Self-Care Development
(Nasal Hygiene)

Code:
  0 No Competency
  1 Moderate Competency
  2 Complete Competency
.... 1. Child does not avoid having his nose cleaned with a tissue.

.... 2. Recognizes the need to clean nose and seeks assistance.

.... 3. Cleans nose with assistance.

.... 4. Tries to clean nose, but is unable to blow nose
properly.

.... 5. Secures a tissue to clean nose independently.

.... 6. Cleans nose independently.

.... Total (max. 12)
Remarks:

Instructional Objective

To have child become aware of the proper use of tissues by playing such games as *this is the way we blow our nose.*

Readiness

Grasps.
Child attends to adult.
Imitates adult's action.
Is not afraid to touch his nose with tissue.

Procedure

1. Seat child.
2. Seat self.
3. Give child tissue.
4. Take tissue yourself and begin singing song such as: This is the way we blow our nose, blow our nose, blow our nose. This is the way we blow our nose, so early in the morning.
5. While singing the song tap the tissue lightly to your face in the area of your nose.
6. If the child doesn't imitate, take his hand and guide him in a light tapping motion while singing.
7. Reward the child appropriately when he imitates your actions.

Task Evaluation

1. Did the child keep the tissue in his hand or did he throw it down or let it fall out as soon as it was given to him?

2. Did he imitate the adult's actions and put the tissue to his face?

3. Did he seem to enjoy the *game* of doing the same thing as the adult?

Materials and Equipment

Chair appropriate size for child
Chair that brings adult to eye level with child
Tissue

Instructional Objective

To have child clean nose with assistance.

Readiness

Grasps.
Child attends to adult.
Imitates adult's action.
Is not afraid to touch his nose with tissue.

Procedure

1. Attract child's attention by saying, (name), let's blow your nose!

2. Take tissue and hand it to child. In a hand over hand method guide his hand to his nose.

3. When he has the tissue at his nose give him the command, (name), blow your nose!

4. If he does not follow through make the blowing sound in hope that he will imitate.

5. Reward any effort on his part to blow his nose.

6. When he has finished command him to throw the tissue away.

7. Make certain that there is a wastebasket nearby and that he disposes of the tissue properly.

Task Evaluation

1. Did child hold tissue after it was given to him?
2. Did he resist the adult's efforts to guide his hand to his nose?
3. Did he understand what he had to do to make the air come through his nose to remove any mucus in the nose?
4. Did he dispose of the tissue properly?

Materials and Equipment

Tissue
Wastebasket

Instructional Objective

To have child communicate need to have nose cleaned to adult.

Readiness

Child realizes that nose is running or that it is stuffed.
Can make gestures known or communicates verbally.
Realizes that adult can help him in relieving the problem of the running or stuffy nose.

Procedure

1. Watch child carefully so that you may note when it is necessary for him to use a tissue.
2. Notice that he may try to clean his running nose with his hand or part of his clothing.
3. When you notice this happening take a tissue to the child and say, (name), blow your nose!
4. Hand the tissue to the child and if necessary guide his hand to his face.
5. It may also be helpful to say to the child when he is seen wiping his nose with his hand, No, no!, (name), use your tissue!

6. If the child is at a lower level, it may be more advantageous to use a single word such as tissue to communicate the command.

Task Evaluation

1. Did you notice that the child often used his hand or clothing to clean his nose?

2. Did he understand that by handing him the tissue that you wanted him to substitute it for cleaning his nose with his hand?

3. Did he begin to realize that it was wrong to clean his nose with his hand and catch himself and ask for a tissue or gesture his need?

Materials and Equipment

Tissues
Wastebasket

Instructional Objective

To have child obtain a tissue when necessary and partially clean his nose with it.

Readiness

Child realizes that nose is running or is stuffed.
Knows where he can obtain tissue.
Partially realizes the process of cleaning his nose.
Child is medically able to keep his mouth closed and blow through his nose.

Procedure

1. When you see that child is in need of tissue, make certain that box is easily accessible to him.

2. If child does not independently go to the tissue box, give him the command, (name), get a tissue!

3. Allow him to make the first attempt at blowing and cleaning his nose.

4. He may not have difficulty wiping his nose clean, so let him

try to do this independently. However, if his nose is stuffed it may require that he blow which he may be unable to do.

5. To teach him how to blow his nose, have him try to blow out a match or candle with his mouth closed. Having him keep his mouth closed is the important factor. Explain that he should take a deep breath while his mouth is closed and then blow keeping his mouth closed.

6. Have the child practice this process several times letting him blow feathers or grains of sugar or salt on a table while keeping his mouth closed.

7. Reward the child appropriately if he has success in blowing his nose.

8. Remind the child that when he is finished with the tissue to dispose of it properly.

Task Evaluation

1. When child felt the need, did he go and obtain a tissue on his own?

2. Did he use the tissue appropriately to wipe his nose?

3. Did the child realize that he had to keep his mouth closed in order to blow the air through his nose?

4. Was child able to remove any of the mucus in his nose by blowing it?

5. Did child know how to dispose of tissue properly?

Materials and Equipment

Tissue
Wastebasket
Candles
Matches
Feathers
Sugar
Salt

Instructional Objective

To have child care for nose independently.

Readiness

Child realizes that nose is running or is stuffed.
Knows where he can obtain tissue.
Realizes the process of blowing his nose.
Knows how and where to dispose of tissue.

Procedure

1. It is the responsibility of the adult to have the box of tissue easily accessible to the child.

2. When you notice that the child is in need of a tissue and he does not seem to realize it, give him the command, (name), blow your nose!

3. Do not go over to assist the child, but let him obtain the tissue himself.

4. Again, give him the command, (name), blow your nose!

5. When he feels that he has finished and his nose is sufficiently clean, command him to throw the tissue away. Show him where the wastebasket is.

6. Go over and praise him appropriately. If there is a serious need for another tissue, help him in a hand over hand method.

7. Avoid discouraging his independence in helping himself.

Task Evaluation

1. Did the child seem to realize on his own that he needed a tissue and secure one, or did he need an adult's reminder?

2. Did he do a sufficient job of cleaning his nose or did it require a further cleaning?

3. If the nose did require more cleaning, did the child seem discouraged that the adult had to help him?

4. Did he respond to the praise that was given to him for his independence?

Materials and Equipment

Tissue
Wastebasket

Competency Checklist

Name _____   Educational Facility _____
Date _____   Educator _____

Instructional Unit
Self-Care Development
(Oral Hygiene)

Code:

0 No Competency
1 Moderate Competency
2 Complete Competency

. . . . 1. Child is not afraid of toothbrush.
. . . . 2. Child becomes accustomed to the taste of toothpaste.
. . . . 3. Child permits adult to brush his teeth.
. . . . 4. Child brushes own teeth with the assistance of
the adult.
. . . . 5. Child brushes teeth with no assistance.
. . . . 6. Child puts toothpaste on brush with assistance.
. . . . 7. Child readies tooth brush and brushes teeth.
. . . . Total (max. 14)
Remarks:

Instructional Objective

To have child become less fearful of toothbrush by playing
games with it.

Readiness

Grasp.
Child directs hand movements.
Child directs arm movements.
Child imitates adult's behavior.

Procedure

1. Seat child.
2. Seat self.
3. Hand the child the toothbrush expecting him to take it with his hand.
4. Take a toothbrush in your hand and begin to imitate the process of brushing the teeth. You may sing: This is the way we brush our teeth, brush our teeth, brush our teeth, this is the way we brush our teeth, so early in the morning. By singing you can make the experience more game like and appealing to the child.
5. If he doesn't begin to imitate your actions, guide his hand in the movement.

Task Evaluation

1. Was child willing to sit and play the tooth brushing game?
2. Did he imitate the adult's actions readily?
3. Did child hold toothbrush appropriately?
4. Would he hold it in close proximity to his mouth?

Materials and Equipment

Child's toothbrush
Toothbrush for adult

Instructional Objective

To have child permit adult to brush his teeth for him, giving the child time to accept the taste of the toothpaste.

Readiness

Child is willing to allow adult to put toothbrush in his mouth.

Child does not gag on the paste or cleaning element on the toothbrush.

Child agreeably keeps his mouth open long enough and wide enough for adult to adequately clean his teeth.

Procedure

1. Attract child by saying, (name), let's brush your teeth!
2. Go to him and accompany him into the bathroom, lead him to the sink.
3. If he is too short to comfortably use the bathroom sink, a small pair of steps should be available for him to stand on.
4. Initially let him taste a small amount of the toothpaste before trying to use it to clean his teeth.
5. If child refuses the taste of the toothpaste, try using a mixture of baking soda and food flavoring (such as orange or cherry flavoring).
6. Do not force the toothbrush into his mouth, let him explore it until he is comfortable with it.
7. Make the process as fast as possible, not demanding that the child keep his mouth open for an extended period of time.

Task Evaluation

1. If child had to use the pair of steps, did he feel secure when standing on them?
2. Did child mind the flavor of the toothpaste?
3. Did he cooperate with the adult by opening his mouth and keeping it open long enough to have his teeth brushed?

Materials and Equipment

Fully equipped bathroom
Child's toothbrush
Small pair steps
Toothpaste or baking soda
Water and flavoring

Instructional Objective

To have child brush his teeth with assistance.

Readiness

Grasp.

Directs arm movements.

Directs hand movements.

Keeps mouth open long enough and wide enough to adequately brush his teeth.

Accepts the texture of the toothbrush and the taste of the toothpaste freely.

Drinks unassisted from cup.

Procedure

1. Attract child by saying, (name), let's brush your teeth!

2. Go to him and accompany him into the bathroom, lead him to the sink.

3. If he is too short to comfortably use the bathroom sink, a small pair of steps should be available for him to stand on.

4. Take child's toothbrush and put a small amount of toothpaste on it.

5. Hand the toothbrush to the child expecting him to take it with his hand.

6. Using a hand over hand method, guide his hand to his mouth.

6. Assist him in moving his hand back and forth over his teeth, trying to force his movements.

8. When you feel that he has sufficiently cleaned his teeth, fill a small cup with water and give it to him asking him to take a drink to rinse the toothpaste from his mouth.

9. If he understands, ask him to take a mouthful of the water and then spit it out and not to swallow the toothpaste.

Task Evaluation

1. Did child maintain good balance while standing in front of the sink on the steps, or floor?

2. Did he grasp the toothbrush?

3. Did he use the toothbrush correctly, moving it back and forth over his teeth?

4. Did he accept the adult's assistance?

5. Did he rinse the toothpaste from his mouth correctly or did he just drink the water from the cup?

Materials and Equipment

Fully equipped bathroom
Child's toothbrush
Toothpaste
Small paper or plastic cup
Water
Small steps

Instructional Objective

To have child put toothpaste on toothbrush with assistance and brush his teeth by himself.

Readiness

Grasp.
Directs arm movements.
Directs hand movements.
Can hold toothbrush steady with hand.
Can exert force in squeezing with hand, thumb and fingers.
Drinks unassisted from cup.

Procedure

1. Attract child by saying, (name), let's brush your teeth!

2. Go to him and accompany him into the bathroom; lead him to the sink.

3. If he is too short to comfortably use the bathroom sink, a small pair of steps should be available for him to stand on.

4. Hand toothbrush to child expecting him to take it with his hand.

5. Hand him the toothpaste. He should take this with his other hand.

6. In a hand over hand manner assist him in squeezing the toothpaste from the tube. He should do this by grasping the tube with the thumb on one side and the four fingers on the other, then squeeze.

7. You should instruct the child to use the toothpaste sparingly.

8. To put the toothpaste on the brush, have the child bring the toothbrush to the opening of the tube of toothpaste. The opening of the tube should be pointed downward.

9. He should hold the toothbrush steady and move the toothpaste from right to left to spread on the brush.

10. When the toothbrush is readied, give him the command, (name), brush your teeth!

11. When he is finished brushing, encourage him to rinse the toothpaste from his mouth by taking a mouthful of water.

Task Evaluation

1. Did the child hold the toothbrush steady with one hand while squeezing the toothpaste with the other?

2. Was the child able to exert enough force with his hand to get some toothpaste out of the tube?

3. Were the child's motions steady enough to hold the toothbrush with one hand and spread the toothpaste with the other?

4. Did he clean and rinse his teeth adequately without the help of the adult?

Materials and Equipment

Fully equipped bathroom
Child's toothbrush
Toothpaste
Small paper or plastic cup
Water
Small steps

Instructional Objective

To have child brush his teeth independently.

Readiness

Grasp.
Directs arm movements.
Directs hand movements.
Can hold toothbrush steady with hand.
Can exert force in squeezing with other hand, thumb and fingers.
Is able to obtain and put toothbrush back in appropriate place.

Procedure

1. Attract the child's attention by saying, (name), let's brush your teeth!
2. Walk into the bathroom expecting him to follow.
3. If the child is too short to comfortably reach bathroom sink, place small pair of steps for the child to stand on.
4. When he is standing at sink, show him where the toothbrush is and command him to take it.
5. When he has the toothbrush, show him where the toothpaste is and command him to take it.
6. Assist him by taking the cap off the tube and hand it to him.
7. Instruct him to put the toothpaste on the brush and then command him to brush his teeth.
8. When they are clean, hand him a cup of water and command him to rinse the toothpaste from his mouth.

Task Evaluation

1. Did the child follow you into the bathroom?
2. Did the child acquire the toothbrush and toothpaste after he was told to get it?
3. Did he follow through after the cap was removed from the toothpaste and put some paste on the toothbrush?
4. Did he clean and rinse his teeth adequately when doing it alone?

Materials and Equipment

Fully equipped bathroom
Child's toothbrush
Toothpaste
Small paper or plastic cup
Water
Small steps

Competency Checklist

Name _____   Educational Facility _____

Date _____   Educator _____

Instructional Unit
Self-Care Development
(Toilet Training)

Code:

0 No Competency
1 Moderate Competency
2 Complete Competency

. . . . 1. Can retain urine for one and one-half to two hours thus allowing use of toilet training program to be implemented.

. . . . 2. Familiar with bathroom.

. . . . 3. Sits on toilet for ten minutes supervised.

. . . . 4. Has sporadic results when on toilet.

. . . . 5. Bowel and bladder control regulated to certain times of the day, regular success on the toilet.

. . . . 6. Gestures toilet needs.

. . . . 7. Moves to toilet unattended.

. . . . 8. Cares for clothing needs in bathroom.

. . . . 9. Cares for personal cleanliness in bathroom.

. . . . 10. Uses toilet appropriately and independently.

. . . . Total (Max. 20)

Remarks:

Instructional Objective

Child is dry for one to two hours permitting a toilet training schedule to be implemented.

Readiness

Child is on a regular schedule for meals.

Eats table food.

Begins to become regular in voiding after meals, bedtime, naps and active play periods.

Child should be ready to wear training pants rather than diapers.

Procedure

1. Take careful notice when child eliminates in pants. This can be done by checking the child every ten minutes for a period of at least five days and marking the results on a chart. The chart should be similar to the one below, or like the chart in the objectives chapter of the text.

9:40—Dry	1:20—Dry
9:20—Wet	1:30—BM & Wet
9:30—Dry	1:40—Dry
9:10—Dry	1:50—Dry

This chart should be readily accessible.

2. When the five-day period is completed, and it is felt that an accurate accounting of the child's eliminating behavior has been obtained, the chart should be analyzed as to the approximate time of day the child eliminates. Similarities in time of day for several days should be noted. If the results are not uniform, this may be an indication that because of the irregularity in eliminating, the child is not yet ready to be put on a toileting schedule.

3. When the chart has been analyzed and specific times of the day are found to be eliminating periods, a schedule for toileting should be made to correspond to the eliminating times. Initially, the child should be placed on the potty every two hours for a ten minute period. The following is an example of an appropriate toilet training schedule:

SUN.

7:15	After Awakening
9:15	After Breakfast
11:15	After Play
1:15	After Lunch
3:15	After Nap
5:15	After Dinner
7:15	After Play
9:15	Before Bed

4. The above schedule allows for the child to be placed on the potty at times when it is most probable that he will eliminate.

Task Evaluation

1. Was there any similarity in the eliminating periods of the child?

2. Did the child void in his pants any more than once every one or two hours?

3. Did you notice if the child voided regularly after meals, naps and vigorous play periods?

Materials and Equipment

Chart with attached pen that measures elimination periods for five days at intervals of ten minutes

Training pants

Instructional Objective

To have child become familiar with bathroom.

Readiness

Child realizes that he has entered different surroundings when taken into the bathroom.

Procedure

1. Before implementing the toilet training program the child should accept the bathroom.

2. To familiarize the child with the bathroom, take him as frequently as possible into the bathroom. This should be done for several days before attempting to have him use the potty.

3. While in this period of adjustment, the adult should explain and demonstrate the different uses of the bathroom.

4. Let the child explore for himself while observing his behavior.

5. By all means the experiences in the bathroom should be pleasant.

Task Evaluation

1. Was child receptive to the bathroom? Did he readily go with the adult when it was suggested?

2. Was he afraid of the bathroom noises—faucets running, toilet flushing?

3. Did he want to explore for himself by flushing the toilet, turning the faucets on and off and examining the potty chair which should be in close proximity to the toilet?

Materials and Equipment

Fully equipped bathroom
Potty chair

Instructional Objective

To have child sit on potty chair with assistance.

Readiness

Able to remain in a sitting position with the assistance of a potty chair guard.

Is aware that bathroom is different than playroom or bedroom.

Freely accepts bathroom atmosphere.

Procedure

1. Attract child's attention by stating, (name), let's go to the potty!

2. Go to child and accompany him into the bathroom.

3. Direct child to potty and assist him in taking pants down.

4. Guide child into a sitting position on the potty.

5. The above three steps should be accompanied with much verbalization on the part of the adult to reassure the child and to calm his fears or doubts about what is occurring in the bathroom.

6. The chair guard should be positioned properly to reassure the child that he is safe in the potty chair.

7. The ten minutes on the potty should be spent supervised by the adult.

8. The ten minute period should not be unpleasant and the child should be kept as interested as possible.

Task Evaluation

1. Did child accept bathroom and potty without undue fear?

2. Did he remain seated on the potty for the ten minute period, or did he try to squeeze out of the chair?

Materials and Equipment

Fully equipped bathroom
Potty chair appropriate for child's size with guard for support
Pants with elastic waistband

Instructional Objective

To have the child relax and achieve results, when placed on the potty.

Readiness

Child's eliminating has been studied and implemented into a toileting schedule.

Procedure

1. Attract the child's attention by saying, (name), let's go to the potty!

2. Go to the child and accompany him to the bathroom.

3. Direct child to the potty and assist him in taking his pants down.

4. Guide child into a sitting position on the potty.

5. Assure the child while on the potty by talking to him and petting him gently.

6. There are various things that can be done to encourage the child to void while on the potty. Some of these are:

   a. Turning on the water faucet in the sink or bathtub, whichever is more visible to the child. The water should run out in a slow stream.

   b. Squirting the child with warm water in the area of the genitals may also aid him in voiding.

   c. Petting the child gently in soft even strokes on the upper thighs or by the genitals may aid in eliminating.

7. Stay close to the child. If he should eliminate, reward him immediately. The reward can be a favorite toy, a piece of sugar coated cereal or something else the child is fond of.

8. Much attention should be given to the fact that the child was successful on the potty.

9. If the child does not eliminate on the potty in the ten minute period, take him off as nonchalantly as possible. Do not praise or scorn.

10. Remember to mark the toilet training chart appropriately in the time slot with either a U for urinate; BM for bowel movement or X for no success.

11. The child may urinate shortly after he has been taken off the potty. This should not be looked at as negative behavior. It very likely shows that the child's bladder muscles are beginning to respond appropriately to sitting on the potty.

Task Evaluation

1. Was the child relaxed on the potty, or did he cry and try to squeeze out of the chair?

2. Did the petting or squirting of water in the area of the genitals aid him in eliminating?

3. If the child was successful, did he seem to realize what he did?

4. Did he connect the reward with voiding in the potty?

Materials and Equipment

Fully equipped bathroom
Potty chair with guard
Squeeze bottle with squirting spout
Toilet training chart
Pants with elastic waistband
Reward appropriate for child

Instructional Objective

To have a child achieve regular success with both bowel and bladder control.

Readiness

Child is able to eat table food and is on a regular schedule for meals.

Child's schedule of eliminating has been charted accurately and employed.

Child will sit on potty for a length of ten minutes.

Procedure

1. Attract child's attention by saying, (name), let's go to the potty!

2. Accompany the child to the bathroom.

3. Direct him to take his pants down by saying, (name), pull your pants down!

4. When his pants are down, give him the command to sit on the potty, (name), sit down!

5. It is necessary to remain with the child during the entire time he is in the bathroom. Immediate reward is essential in toilet training. Listen for the child to eliminate and reward immediately, saying good boy, (name), you made wee-wee or another word that the child associates with eliminating. It is important for the child to realize why he is being rewarded.

6. If the child does not eliminate when on the potty, take him off, neither scorning nor rewarding him. However if the child should eliminate in his pants, change him immediately and do not place any emphasis on the matter at all. The experience should not be pleasant nor a drawn out scorning session. Just change the child and say nothing.

7. For the child to be successful, it is necessary that the instructor be fair and remember the child's schedule. Take him to the bathroom at appropriate times and as often as necessary.

8. Give the child incentive to eliminate on the potty by verbally reinforcing his successful behavior and showing him that you are going to give him a star on the chart. The toileting chart should be marked in front of the child when he achieves success.

Task Evaluation

1. Does the child seem to have a regular pattern for bowel movement and voiding daily?

2. Does he relax on the potty and eliminate soon after he is placed on it?

3. When he does have an eliminating accident, does he seem to realize that he has behaved inappropriately?

Materials and Equipment

Fully equipped bathroom
Potty chair
Toilet training chart
Pants with elastic waistband
Appropriate reward

Instructional Objective

To have child begin to communicate toilet needs.

Readiness

Child begins to recognize feeling of having to eliminate.
Begins to associate or gesture bathroom needs.
Child is in the early stages of communication.

Procedure

1. Become aware of any gestures or words that the child uses before he eliminates.

2. Observe your words and actions when asking the child if he has to go to the potty. You will be looking for the repeated use of a word or gesture.

3. When you feel that the child is consistently using a word or action before he eliminates or while he is going to the bathroom, use the word or action in every encounter involving the bathroom. *Overuse* the word or gesture when the child is on the potty or when you first approach the child to take him to the bathroom.

4. Before taking the child into the bathroom use his word or gesture to communicate what you want.

Remember to reward the child if he uses a word or gesture in association with the bathroom. He is building a means of communicating his needs. This is progress.

Task Evaluation

1. After using the same command consistently when taking the child to the bathroom, did he realize where he was going?

2. Did child hold himself or touch his genitals before eliminating?

3. Did he try to repeat a word spoken by the instructor while he was on the potty?

Materials and Equipment

Fully equipped bathroom
Potty chair
Toilet training chart
Pants with elastic waistband
Reward appropriate for child

Instructional Objective

To have child go to the bathroom unattended.

Readiness

Child begins to associate the command with the toileting function.

Child begins to associate the need to eliminate with going to the bathroom.

Child relies on the presence of the instructor in the bathroom.

Child is able to move independently, either by walking, crawling or creeping.

Procedure

1. Observe the toilet training schedule attending to the child's verbalizations and gestures. Notice when it is time for the child to use the bathroom.

2. Attract child's attention by saying, (name), go to the potty!

3. Do not assist the child into the bathroom, but walk toward the area expecting the child to follow.

4. If necessary, encourage child by repeating the command.

5. When the child accomplishes the task of following to the bathroom, proceed to the next step.

6. Give the child the command, (name), go to the potty! This time do not go to the bathroom first, but let the child go alone. You may follow.

7. The final goal is to have the child become independent in going to the bathroom when he has the need.

8. It may be good to try and follow a schedule of going to the bathroom that is consistent in time. The child may associate going to the bathroom with the completion of an activity, for example, after lunch period.

Task Evaluation

1. How soon did the child begin to associate the command with the action?

2. Did he appear afraid or reluctant to go into the bathroom without your accompanying him?

3. Did he begin to develop independence in this task and go toward the bathroom without the command?

Materials and Equipment

Fully equipped bathroom
Potty chair
Toilet training chart
Pants with elastic waistband
Reward appropriate for child

Instructional Objective

To have child care for clothing in bathroom.

Readiness

Grasp.
Directs arm movements.
Directs hand movements.

Procedure

1. Attract child's attention by saying, (name), go to the potty or bathroom! Use any term the child understands to begin with. The word bathroom should be used eventually.

2. Wait for the child to go into the bathroom independently, then follow.

3. When child is near potty chair or toilet, give him the command, (name), pull down your pants!

4. If necessary, guide the child's hands to the waistband of his pants. Using a hand over hand method, have the child grasp the waistband of his pants on both sides.

5. Instruct child to push his outer pants down to knee level. He should do the same with his underpants. Girls should wear slacks. If the girl has a dress on, instruct her to grasp the sides and lift up.

6. When child has taken care of his clothing, instruct him to sit on the toilet. If child is small use the potty chair. Boys should be instructed to hold penis down with hand.

7. When the child has finished using the toilet, give the command to stand and pull pants up. Instruct him to bend at waist, grasp underpants at waistband and pull up into position. Repeat with outer pants.

Task Evaluation

1. Did child maintain good grasp on waistband of pants?
2. Was child's balance good when pushing pants down?
3. Was the female able to hold dress up while pushing down her underpants?
4. Was the child able to use the toilet rather than the potty?
5. Was child able to bring pants back into position?

Materials and Equipment

Fully equipped bathroom
Potty chair
Toilet training chart
Pants with elastic waistband
Reward appropriate for child

Instructional Obective

To have child care for personal cleanliness in bathroom.

Readiness

Grasps.
Directs arm movements.
Directs hand movements.
Child realizes reasons for washing and cleaning himself.

Procedure

1. Attract child's attention by saying, (name), go to the bathroom!
2. Wait for the child to go independently, then follow.

3. When in the area of the toilet or potty chair, give him the command, (name), pull down your pants!

4. When he has taken care of his clothing, instruct him to sit down on the toilet. Smaller children may use the potty chair. Boys should be instructed to hold penis down with hand.

5. When child has eliminated, guide his hand to the toilet tissue holder. Using a hand over hand method have him spin the roll of tissue so that some comes off the roll.

6. Direct the child to tear the paper with one hand and wrap around his fingers.

7. Direct the child's hand downward and backward in wiping himself clean.

8. Guide his hand as often as necessary.

9. Instruct the child to drop the tissue into the toilet and obtain clean tissue, if needed.

10. When child has positioned pants, command him to wash his hands.

Task Evaluation

1. Was child able to manipulate the toilet tissue roll to make the tissue come off?

2. Was child able to tear toilet tissue from the roll and maintain balance while on the toilet?

3. Was he able to wrap toilet tissue around his hand?

4. Was child able to clean himself?

Materials and Equipment

Fully equipped bathroom
Potty chair
Toilet training chart
Pants with elastic waistband
Reward appropriate for child

Instructional Objective

To have child use toilet appropriately and independently.

Readiness

Child realizes the need to eliminate.
He is able to move to bathroom independently or communicate need.
Is able to care for clothing in bathroom.
Can take care of personal cleanliness.

Procedure

1. Child enters bathroom on command or independently.
2. Child takes outer and underpants down and sits on the toilet.
3. When finished eliminating, the child should tear toilet tissue and clean himself thoroughly and release the dirty tissue into the toilet.
4. When clean he should stand and pull his pants up.
5. When clothing is in place, have child flush the toilet.
6. If necessary, guide the child's hand over the lever and assist him in releasing the lever. It should be stressed that the lever is not a toy and is only used when he eliminates successfully.
7. When he has accomplished the task, direct him to the sink and aid, if necessary, in washing his hands.

Task Evaluation

1. Was the child able to independently take care of himself in the bathroom?
2. Was he able, with assistance, to flush toilet?
3. Was the child able to complete the toileting function by cleaning his hands?

Materials and Equipment

Fully equipped bathroom
Potty chair
Toilet training chart
Pants with elastic waistband
Reward appropriate for child

Competency Checklist

Name _____   Educational Facility_____

Date _____   Educator_____

Instructional Unit
Self-Care Development
(Dressing)

Code:

0 No Competency

1 Moderate Competency

2 Complete Competency

.... 1. Child pulls sock off when it is just over his toes.

.... 2. Child pulls sock off when it is placed at his mid-foot.

.... 3. Child pulls sock off when it is positioned at the heel.

.... 4. Child pulls sock off when it is around the ankle.

.... 5. Child removes sock independently.

.... 6. Child pulls sock on from ankles.

.... 7. Child pulls sock on from heel.

.... 8. Child pulls sock on from mid-foot

.... 9. Child pulls sock on from when they have been placed just over his toes.

.... 10. Child puts sock on independently.

.... 11. Child takes pants off when just one foot is in pant leg and the pants are down by ankles.

.... 12. Takes pants off when both feet are in pant legs and pants are down by ankles.

.... 13. Takes pants off when they are by his knees.

.... 14. Takes pants off when they are positioned by hips.

.... 15. Takes pants off independently.

.... 16. Pulls pants on when they are by his hips.

.... 17. Pulls pants up from knees.

.... 18. Pulls pants up from ankles.

.... 19. Puts one foot in pant leg and pulls pants up.

.... 20. Puts pants on independently.

.... 21. Removes shirt when it is sitting on top of his head.

.... 22. Removes shirt when it is at eye level on his face.

.... 23. Removes shirt when it is around his neck.

.... 24. Releases one arm from the armhole and pulls the shirt up and over his head.

.... 25. Releases both arms from the armholes and pulls shirt up and over his head.

.... 26. Child removes shirt when it is placed at mid-stomach.

.... 27. Removes shirt independently.

.... 28. Pulls shirt down from mid-stomach.

.... 29. Pulls shirt down from under armpits.

.... 30. Puts one arm in armhole and pulls shirt into position.

.... 31. Puts both arms in armholes and pulls shirt into position.

.... 32. Pulls shirt down from eye level, puts both arms in armholes and pulls shirt into position.

.... 33. Puts shirt on independently.

.... 34. Takes shoes off when only tips of toes are in them.

.... 35. Takes shoes off when heel and back part of foot are released from shoe.

.... 36. Takes shoe off independently.

.... 37. Puts shoe on by pushing heel into proper position.

.... 38. Puts shoe on when heel is completely out of shoe.

.... 39. Puts shoe on when just tips of toes are in shoe.

.... 40. Puts shoe on independently.

.... 41. Takes hat off when it is sitting on the top of his head.

.... 42. Takes hat off when it is pulled halfway into position.

.... 43. Takes hat off independently.

.... 44. Puts hat on when it is placed halfway on head.

.... 45. Puts hat on when it is sitting on top of his head.

.... 46. Puts hat on independently.

.... 47. Removes mitten when thumb is released and mitten is only partially on four fingers.

.... 48. Removes mitten when it is halfway over thumb and positioned properly over four fingers.

.... 49. Takes mitten off independently.

.... 50. Puts mitten on when thumb and four fingers are positioned in it properly and mitten is halfway on.

.... 51. Puts mitten on when it is only one fourth of the way on.

.... 52. Puts mitten on independently.

.... 53. Can take coat off when hand and arm are released from sleeve and coat is sitting on shoulder.

.... 54. Takes coat off independently.

.... 55. Puts coat on by pushing arm and hand through armhole when positioned at armhole and rest of coat is positioned.

.... 56. Puts coat on by bringing arm around back to armhole of coat, placing arm and hand in armhole and bringing coat into proper position.

.... 57. Puts coat on when it is held for him at side.

.... 58. Puts coat on independently.

.... 59. Unsnaps when hands are positioned properly.

.... 60. Unsnaps independently.

.... 61. Snaps when top snap is positioned on bottom but not fastened.

.... 62. Snaps independently.

.... 63. Unzips zipper when zipper is three quarters of the way down.

.... 64. Unzips when zipper is halfway down.

.... 65. Unzips independently.

.... 66. Zips when zipper is three quarters of the way up.

.... 67. Zips when zipper is halfway up.

.... 68. Zips when zipper is one fourth the way up.

.... 69. Zips independently.

.... 70. Unbuttons when button is three quarters of the way through buttonhole.

.... 71. Unbuttons when button is halfway through buttonhole.

.... 72. Unbuttons independently.

.... 73. Buttons when button is three quarters of the way through the buttonhole.

.... 74. Buttons when button is halfway through buttonhole.

.... 75. Buttons independently.

.... Total (Max. 150)

Remarks:

Instructional Objective

To have child successfully pull sock off when it is just over his toes.

Readiness

Grasp.

Child directs arm movements.

Child directs hand movements.

Child directs foot movements.

Child directs leg movements.

Child can compensate for any move to right or left, forward or backward while in a sitting position.

Procedure

1. Sit child on chair.
2. Sit on chair.
3. Place sock just over toes.
4. Give him the command, (name), take your sock off!
5. Direct child to bend at waist and grasp the end of the sock.
6. Encourage him to pull sock off. If necessary, use hand over hand method of instruction.
7. Repeat steps 4, 5 and 6 until child is consistently successful.

Task Evaluation

1. Did child maintain good balance when bending over to grasp the sock?
2. Did he grasp the sock firmly or did it just keep slipping from his hand?
3. Did he pull the sock off in a smooth motion?
4. How long did it take the child to become consistently successful?

Materials and Equipment

Chair appropriate to child's size
Chair for instructor that enables him to be at eye level with the
    child
Sock slightly larger than what the child might normally wear

Instructional Objective

To have child successfully pull sock off when it is at his mid-foot.

Readiness

Grasp.
Child directs arm movements.
Child directs hand movements.

Child directs foot movements.

Child directs leg movements.

Child can compensate for any move to right or left, forward or backward while in a sitting position.

Procedure

1. Sit child on chair.
2. Sit on chair.
3. Place sock at mid-foot.
4. Give him the command, (name), take your sock off!
5. Direct the child to bend at the waist and grasp the end of the sock (four fingers on the bottom of the sock, thumb on the top). This should be done with dominant hand.
6. Encourage him to pull off sock, using a hand over hand method of instruction, if necessary.
7. Repeat steps 4, 5 and 6 until child is consistently successful.

Task Evaluation

1. Did child maintain good balance when bending over to grasp the sock?
2. Did he grasp the sock firmly or did it just keep slipping from his hand?
3. Did he pull the sock off in a smooth motion?
4. How long did it take the child to become consistently successful?

Materials and Equipment

Chair appropriate to child's size

Chair for instructor that enables him to be at eye level with the child

Sock slightly larger than what the child might normally wear

Instructional Objective

To have child successfully pull sock off when at the heel position.

Readiness

Grasp.
Child directs arm movements.
Child directs hand movements.
Child directs foot movements.
Child directs leg movements.
Child can compensate for any move to right or left, forward or backward while in a sitting position.

Procedure

1. Sit child on chair.
2. Sit on chair.
3. Place sock at heel position.
4. Give him the command, (name), take your sock off!
5. Direct the child to bend at the waist and grasp the end of the sock (four fingers on the outside and thumb on the inside between the foot and sock). This procedure is for both hands which should be grasping the sock.
6. The child should be instructed to push the sock off the foot. Use a hand over hand method of instruction, if necessary.
7. Repeat steps 4, 5 and 6 until the child is consistently successful.

Task Evaluation

1. Did child maintain good balance when bending over to grasp the sock?
2. Did he grasp the sock firmly or did it just keep slipping from his hand?
3. Did he pull the sock off in a smooth motion?
4. Did child display any trouble in pushing the sock over the heel?
5. How long did it take the child to become consistently successful?

Materials and Equipment

Chair appropriate to child's size

Chair for instructor that enables him to be at eye level with
the child
Sock slightly larger than what the child might normally wear

Instructional Objective

To have child successfully pull sock off when it is at the ankle
position.

Readiness

Grasp.
Child directs arm movements.
Child directs hand movements.
Child directs foot movements.
Child directs leg movements.
Child can compensate for any move to right or left, forward
or backward while in a sitting position.

Procedure

1. Sit child on chair.
2. Sit on chair.
3. Place sock at ankle position.
4. Give him the command, (name), take your sock off!
5. Direct the child to bend at the waist and grasp the top of
the sock with both hands. Four fingers on the outside and thumb
on the inside between the foot and sock.
6. Direct him to push the sock down and over the heel and
then off the foot.
7. Repeat steps 4, 5 and 6 until child is consistently successful.

Task Evaluation

1. Did child maintain good balance when bending over to
grasp the sock?
2. Did he grasp the sock firmly or did it just keep slipping
from his hand?

3. Did he pull the sock off in a smooth motion?
4. Did child exhibit any problem in grasping the sock and pushing it off the foot?
5. How long did it take the child to become consistently successful?

Materials and Equipment

Chair appropriate to child's size
Chair for instructor that enables him to be at eye level with the child
Sock slightly larger than what the child might normally wear

Instructional Objective

To have child remove sock independently.

Readiness

Grasp.
Child directs arm movements.
Child directs hand movements.
Child directs foot movements.
Child directs leg movements.
Child can compensate for any move to right or left, forward or backward while in a sitting position.

Procedure

1. Seat child on chair.
2. Sit on chair.
3. Put sock on entirely.
4. Give him the command, (name), take your sock off!
5. Direct the child to bend at the waist and grasp the top of the sock with both hands (four fingers on the outside, thumb on the inside) between foot and sock.

6. Direct him to push the sock down and over the heel and then off the foot.

7. Repeat steps 4, 5 and 6 until child is consistently successful.

Task Evaluation

1. Did child maintain good balance when bending over to grasp the sock?

2. Did he grasp the sock firmly or did it just keep slipping from his hand?

3. Did he pull the sock off in a smooth motion?

4. Did child display any trouble in pushing the sock over the heel?

5. How long did it take the child to become consistently successful?

Materials and Equipment

Chair appropriate to child's size

Chair for instructor that enables him to be at eye level with the child

Sock slightly larger than what the child might normally wear

Instructional Objective

To have child successfully pull socks on from ankle position.

Readiness

Grasp.

Child directs arm movements.

Child directs hand movements.

Child directs foot movements.

Child directs leg movements.

Can compensate for any move to right or left, forward or backward, while in a sitting position.

Procedure

1. Seat child on chair.
2. Sit on chair.
3. Place sock at ankle position.
4. Give him the command, (name), put your sock on!
5. Direct the child to bend over at the waist and grasp the top of the sock with both hands (four fingers on the outside of the sock, thumb on the inside).
6. Direct the child to pull the sock into position. If necessary, use a hand over hand method of instruction.
7. Repeat steps 4, 5 and 6 until the child is consistently successful.

Task Evaluation

1. Did child maintain good balance when bending over to grasp sock?
2. Did he grasp the sock firmly or did it just keep slipping out of his hands?
3. Did he pull the sock up in a smooth motion or did he pull and tug at it?
4. How long did it take the child to become consistently successful?

Materials and Equipment

Chair appropriate size for child
Chair for instructor that enables him to be eye level with the child
Sock slightly larger than what the child might wear

Instructional Objective

To have child successfully pull sock on from heel position.

Readiness

Grasp.
Child directs arm movements.

Child directs hand movements.
Child directs foot movements.
Child directs leg movements.
Can compensate for any move to right or left, forward or backward, while in a sitting position.

Procedure

1. Seat child on chair.
2. Sit on chair.
3. Place sock at heel position.
4. Give command, (name), put your sock on!
5. Direct the child to bend over at the waist and grasp the top of the sock with both hands (four fingers on the outside, thumb on the inside).
6. Instruct the child to pull the sock over the heel and up into place. Use a hand over hand method of instruction if necessary.
7. Repeat steps 4, 5 and 6 until the child is consistently successful.

Task Evaluation

1. Did child maintain good balance when bending over to grasp sock?
2. Did he grasp the sock firmly or did it just keep slipping out of his hands?
3. Did he pull the sock up in a smooth motion or did he pull and tug at it?
4. How long did it take the child to become consistently successful?

Materials and Equipment

Chair appropriate size for child
Chair for instructor that enables him to be eye level with the child
Sock slightly larger than what the child might wear

Instructional Objective

To have child successfully pull socks on from mid-foot position.

Readiness

Grasp.
Child directs arm movements.
Child directs hand movements.
Child directs foot movements.
Child directs leg movements.
Can compensate for any move to right or left, forward or backward, while in a sitting position.

Procedure

1. Seat child on chair.
2. Sit on chair.
3. Place sock at mid-foot position.
4. Give him the command, (name), put your sock on!
5. Direct the child to bend over at the waist and grasp the top of the sock with both hands (four fingers on the outside of the sock, thumb on the inside).
6. Instruct him to pull the sock to the heel and then over the heel and up into position. Use hand over hand method of instruction if necessary.
7. Repeat steps 4, 5 and 6 until child is consistently successful.

Task Evaluation

1. Did child maintain good balance when bending over to grasp sock?
2. Did he grasp the sock firmly or did it just keep slipping out of his hands?
3. Did he pull the sock up in a smooth motion or did he pull and tug at it?
4. Did child exhibit any difficulty in pulling the sock over the heel?

5. How long did it take the child to become consistently successful?

Materials and Equipment

Chair appropriate size for child
Chair for instructor that enables him to be eye level with the child
Sock slightly larger than what the child might wear

Instructional Objective

To have child successfully pull socks on from just over toe position.

Readiness

Grasp.
Child directs arm movements.
Child directs hand movements.
Child directs foot movements.
Child directs leg movements.
Can compensate for any move to right or left, forward or backward, while in a sitting position.

Procedure

1. Seat child on chair.
2. Sit on chair.
3. Place sock just over toes.
4. Give him the command, (name), put your socks on!
5. Direct the child to bend over at the waist and grasp the top of the sock with both hands (four fingers on the outside and thumb on the inside).
6. Instruct the child to pull the sock to the heel and then over the heel and up into position. Use hand over hand method of instruction if necessary.

7. Repeat steps 4, 5 and 6 until the child is consistently successful.

Task Evaluation

1. Did child maintain good balance when bending over to grasp sock?
2. Did he grasp the sock firmly or did it just keep slipping out of his hands?
3. Did he pull the sock up in a smooth motion or did he pull and tug at it?
4. How long did it take the child to become consistently successful?

Materials and Equipment

Chair appropriate size for child
Chair for instructor that enables him to be eye level with the
    child
Sock slightly larger than what the child might wear

Instructional Objective

To have child successfully pull sock on independently.

Readiness

Grasp.
Child directs arm movements.
Child directs hand movements.
Child directs foot movements.
Child directs leg movements.
Can compensate for any move to right or left, forward or backward, while in a sitting position.

Procedure

1. Seat child on chair.
2. Sit on chair.

3. Hold the sock open by the grasp method that has been described earlier, four fingers on outside of sock, thumb on inside, both hands holding the sock.

4. Give child the command, (name), put your sock on!

5. Direct the child to grasp the sock in the same manner as was described in step three.

6. Direct him to bend at the waist and slightly lift his foot to slide it into the open end of the sock.

7. He should then pull the sock to the heel and then over the heel.

8. Repeat steps 4, 5, 6 and 7 until the child is consistently successful.

Task Evaluation

1. Did child maintain good balance when bending over to grasp sock?

2. Did he grasp the sock firmly or did it just keep slipping out of his hands?

3. Did he pull the sock up in a smooth motion or did he pull and tug at it?

4. Did child exhibit any problems in lifting his foot and sliding it into the sock? Did he maintain his balance when going through this step?

5. Was child able to hold sock top open until he got it down by his foot?

6. How long did it take the child to become consistently successful?

Materials and Equipment

Chair appropriate size for child

Chair for instructor that enables him to be eye level with the child

Sock slightly larger than what the child might wear

Instructional Objective

To have child successfully take pants off when one foot is in pant leg and pants are at the ankle position.

Readiness

Grasp.
Directs arm movements.
Directs hand movements.
Can compensate for any move to the right or left, forward or backward, while in a sitting position.
Directs foot movements.
Directs leg movements.

Procedure

1. Place child in a sitting position.
2. Place pants over one foot to ankle to leave the foot free.
3. Sit on chair that brings you to eye level with child.
4. Give him the command, (name), take your pants off!
5. Direct the child to bend at the waist and grasp the pants around his foot. If necessary, use a hand over hand method to teach him to grasp the pants.
6. When the child has grasped the pants, encourage him to lift his foot and pull the pants off.
7. Repeat steps 4, 5 and 6 until the child is consistently successful.

Task Evaluation

1. Did child maintain good balance when bending over to grasp his pants?
2. Did he maintain good balance when lifting his foot to pull the pants off?
3. Did he pull the pants off in a smooth motion, or did he pull and tug to get them off?
4. How many times did you have to repeat steps 4, 5 and 6 before the child was consistently successful?

Materials and Equipment

Chair for child appropriate for his size
Chair that brings instructor to eye level with child
A pair of slacks with elastic waist band larger than what the
child would normally wear

Instructional Objective

To have child successfully take pants off when both feet are
in pant legs and pants are at the ankle position.

Readiness

Grasp.
Directs arm movements.
Directs hand movements.
Can compensate for any move to the right or left, forward or
backward, while in a sitting position.
Directs foot movements.
Directs leg movements.

Procedure

1. Place child in a sitting position.
2. Place pants over both feet and at ankle length.
3. Sit on chair that brings you to eye level with child.
4. Give him the command, (name), take your pants off!
5. Direct the child to bend at the waist and grasp the pants
around his feet. If necessary, use a hand over hand method to
teach him to grasp the pants.
6. When the child has grasped his pants, encourage him to first
lift his foot straight up and pull the pants off. He then should
place the foot on the floor for support and lift the other foot
and pull the pants entirely off.
7. Repeat steps 4, 5 and 6 until the child is consistently successful.

Task Evaluation

1. Did child maintain good balance when bending over to grasp his pants?
2. Did he maintain good balance when lifting his feet to pull the pants off?
3. Did he pull the pants off in a smooth motion or did he pull and tug to get them off?
4. How many times did you repeat steps 4, 5 and 6 before the child was consistently successful?

Materials and Equipment

Chair for child appropriate for his size
Chair that brings instructor to eye level with child
A pair of slacks with elastic waist band, larger than what the child would normally wear

Instructional Objective

To have child successfully take pants off when they are at the knee position.

Readiness

Grasp.
Directs arm movement.
Directs hand movements.
Can maintain balance when bending over while in a standing position.
Directs foot movements.
Direct leg movements.

Procedure

1. Place child in a standing position.
2. Position pants at child's knees.
3. Sit on chair.

4. Give him the command, (name), take your pants off!

5. Instruct child to bend over and push the pants down to his ankles. If necessary, use a hand over hand method.

6. When he has the pants down by his ankles, encourage him to sit down on chair.

7. When sitting, direct him to bend at the waist and grasp the pants that are around his ankles. If necessary, again use a hand over hand method.

8. Now encourage him to lift his foot straight up and pull the pants off. He then should place the foot on the floor for support, lift the other foot and pull the pants entirely off.

9. Repeat steps 4 through 8 until the child is consistently successful.

Task Evaluation

1. Did child maintain good balance when bending over in a standing position to push the pants down?

2. Did he maintain good balance when bending over in the sitting position to grasp the pants?

3. Did he remain steady when lifting his feet to pull them out of the pant legs?

4. Did he pull the pants down and off in a smooth motion, or did he pull and tug to get them off?

5. How many times did you have to repeat the procedure before the child was consistently successful?

Materials and Equipment

Chair that brings instructor to eye level with child
Chair for child appropriate for his size
A pair of slacks with elastic waist band larger than what the child would normally wear

Instructional Objective

To have child successfully take pants off when they are at the hip position.

Readiness

Grasp.
Directs arm movements.
Directs hand movements.
Can maintain balance when bending over while in a standing position.
Can move from a standing to a sitting position.
Directs foot movements.
Directs leg movements.

Procedure

1. Place child in a standing position.
2. Position pants at child's hips.
3. Sit on chair.
4. Give him the command, (name), take your pants off!
5. Instruct the child to put his hands on the waist band in a grasping manner (four fingers on the outside, thumb on the inside) and push them down to the ankles, bending as he does it.
6. When he has pants down at ankles, encourage him to sit down on a chair.
7. When sitting, direct him to bend at the waist and grasp the pants that are around his ankles. If necessary, use hand over hand method of instruction.
8. Encourage him to lift his foot straight up and pull the pants off. He should place the foot on the floor for support, lift the other foot and pull the pants entirely off.
9. Repeat steps 4 through 8 until the child is consistently successful.

Task Evaluation

1. Did child maintain good balance when bending over in a standing position to push the pants down?
2. Did he maintain good balance when bending over in the sitting position to grasp the pants?
3. Did he remain steady when lifting his feet to pull them out of the pant legs?

4. Did he pull the pants down and off in a smooth motion or did he pull and tug to get them off?

5. How many times did you have to repeat the procedure before the child was consistently successful?

Materials and Equipment

Chair for child appropriate for his size

Chair that brings instructor to eye level with child

A pair of slacks with elastic waist band larger than what the child would normally wear

Instructional Objective

To have child successfully take pants off independently.

Readiness

Grasp.

Directs arm movements.

Directs hand movements.

Can maintain balance when bending over while in a standing position.

Can move from a standing to a sitting position.

Directs foot movements.

Direct leg movements.

Procedure

1. Place child in a standing position.
2. Position pants at child's waist.
3. Sit on chair.
4. Give him the command, (name), take your pants off!
5. Instruct the child to put his hands on the waist band in a grasping manner (four fingers on outside, thumb on inside) and push the pants down to the ankles, bending as he does it.
6. When he has the pants down by his ankles, encourage him to sit down.

7. When sitting, direct him to bend at the waist and grasp the pants that are around his ankles. If necessary, use hand over hand instruction.

8. Encourage him to lift his foot, straight up and pull the pants off. He then should place the foot on the floor for support, lift the other foot and pull the pants off entirely.

9. Repeat steps 4 through 8 until the child is consistently successful.

Task Evaluation

1. Did child maintain good balance when bending over in a standing position to push the pants down?

2. Did he maintain good balance when bending over in the sitting position to grasp the pants?

3. Did he remain steady when lifting his feet to pull them out of the pant legs?

4. Did he pull the pants down and off in a smooth motion or did he pull and tug to get them off?

5. How many times did you have to repeat the procedure before the child was consistently successful?

Materials and Equipment

Chair that brings instructor to eye level with child
Chair for child appropriate for his size
A pair of slacks with elastic waist band larger than what the child would normally wear

Instructional Objective

To have child successfully pull pants up from hip position.

Readiness

Grasp.
Directs arm movements.
Directs hand movements.
Maintains a stand.

Procedure

1. Pull slacks to child's hips.
2. Command child to stand up; aid him if necessary.
3. Seat child on chair that brings you to eye level with him.
4. Give him the command, (name), put your pants on!
5. Place child's hands on the waist band of the pants by his hips. His four fingers should be on the outside, thumb on the inside.
6. In a hand over hand manner, help the child to pull the pants into position.
7. Repeat steps 4, 5 and 6 until the child is consistently successful.

Task Evaluation

1. Did the child grasp the waist band of the pants firmly or did they keep slipping out of his hands?
2. Did he bring his pants up in a smooth motion or did he pull and tug at them?
3. How long did it take before the child was consistently successful?

Materials and Equipment

Chair that brings instructor to eye level with child
Chair for child appropriate for his size
A pair of slacks with elastic waist band larger than what the child would normally wear

Instructional Objective

To have child successfully pull pants up from knee position.

Readiness

Grasp.
Directs arm movements.

Directs hand movements.

Maintains a stand.

Maintains balance while in a bending position.

Procedure

1. Pull pants to child's knees.
2. Command him to stand up; aid him if necessary.
3. Sit on chair that brings you to eye level with child.
4. Give him the command, (name), put your pants on!
5. Instruct the child to bend at the waist to grasp the waist band of the pants. Aid him if necessary by applying slight pressure to his back.
6. Place child's hands on the waist band of the pants which are down by his knees. His four fingers should be on the outside of the pants while the thumb is on the inside.
7. In a hand over hand method help the child to pull his pants into position.
8. Repeat steps 4 through 7 until the child is consistently successful.

Task Evaluation

1. Did the child maintain good balance while he was bending over to pull up his pants?
2. Did he grasp the waist band firmly or did it keep slipping out of his hands?
3. Did he bring his pants up in a smooth motion or did he pull and tug at them?
4. How long did it take before the child was consistently successful?

Materials and Equipment

Chair that brings instructor to eye level with child

Chair for child appropriate for his size

A pair of slacks with elastic waist band larger than what the child would normally wear

Instructional Objective

To have child successfully pull pants up from ankle position.

Readiness

Grasp.
Directs arm movements.
Directs hand movements.
Maintains a stand.
Maintains balance while in a bending position.

Procedure

1. Put child's pants on just to ankles.
2. Command him to stand up; aid if necessary.
3. Sit on chair that brings you to eye level with child.
4. Give him the command, (name), put your pants on!
5. Instruct the child to bend at the waist to grasp the waist band. Aid him if necessary by applying slight pressure to his back.
6. Place child's hands on the waist band of the pants which are down by his ankles. He should grasp in this manner: four fingers on the outside of the pants, thumb on the inside.
7. In a hand over hand method help the child to pull his pants into position.
8. Repeat steps 4 through 7 until the child is consistently successful.

Task Evaluation

1. Did the child grasp the waist band of the pants firmly or did they keep slipping out of his hands?
2. Did he bring his pants up in a smooth motion or did he pull and tug at them?
3. How long did it take before the child was consistently successful?

Materials and Equipment

Chair that brings instructor to eye level with child
Chair for child appropriate for his size

A pair of slacks with elastic waist band larger than what the child would normally wear

Instructional Objective

To have child successfully put one foot in pant leg and pull pants up.

Readiness

Grasp.
Directs arm movements.
Directs hand movements.
Maintains a stand.
Can move from a sitting to a standing position.
Directs leg movements.
Directs foot movements.

Procedure

1. Seat child.
2. Put pant leg over one foot.
3. Sit on chair that brings you to eye level with child.
4. Give him the command, (name), put your pants on!
5. Instruct child to bend at the waist and grasp the waist band of the pants with the four fingers on the outside and the thumb on the inside. Aid him if necessary by giving him a gentle push on the back to bend over.
6. He should then be instructed to lift the free leg and place his foot in the free pant leg. Aid him in this step if necessary by giving his leg a small lift.
7. He should then be instructed to stand up and be given the command, (name), put your pants on!
8. He will have to bend at the waist, grasp the waist band in the method that was explained above and pull the pants up from the ankles.
9. Steps 4 through 8 should be repeated until the child is consistently successful.

Task Evaluation

1. Did the child maintain good balance while bending over from a sitting position as well as the standing position?
2. Was the child able to bring himself to a stand from the sitting position?
3. Did he maintain good balance while lifting his free leg to place it in the pant leg?
4. Did he grasp the waist band firmly, or did it keep slipping out of his hands?
5. Did he bring his pants up in a smooth motion or did he pull and tug at them?
6. How long did it take before the child was consistently successful?

Materials and Equipment

Chair that brings instructor to eye level with child

Chair for child appropriate for his size

A pair of slacks with elastic waist band larger than what the child would normally wear

Instructional Objective

To have child put pants on independently.

Readiness

Grasp.

Directs arm movements.

Directs hand movements.

Maintains a stand.

Can move from a sitting to a standing position.

Directs leg movements.

Directs foot movements.

Procedure

1. Seat child on chair.
2. Hand him pants, holding the waist band.

3. Direct the child to place his hands on the waist band and stretch it open grasping it as explained earlier, four fingers on the outside, thumb on the inside.

4. When he has stretched open the top of the pants, guide his arms down to his feet.

5. Direct him to first lift his foot and put it in the pant leg and then the other.

6. When he has both feet in the pant legs and they are around his ankles, he should stand up.

7. When standing the child should be directed to bend down and pull up the pants by the waist band.

Task Evaluation

1. Did the child maintain good balance while bending over from a sitting position as well as the standing position?

2. Was the child able to bring himself to a stand from a sitting position?

3. Did he maintain good balance when lifting his legs to put them in the pant legs?

4. Did he grasp the waist band firmly or did it keep slipping out of his hands?

5. Did he bring his pants up in a smooth motion or did he pull and tug at them?

6. How long did it take before the child was consistently successful?

Materials and Equipment

Chair that brings instructor to eye level with child
Chair for child appropriate for his size
A pair of slacks with elastic waist band larger than what the
child would normally wear

Instructional Objective

To have child remove shirt when it is on top of his head.

Readiness

Grasp.
Directed arm movements.
Directed hand movements.

Procedure

1. Place the child in a sitting position.
2. Place the shirt on top of the child's head.
3. Give him the command, (name), take your shirt off!
4. If the child does not respond, move his hand to the top of his head, and using a hand over hand method, aid him in grasping the shirt and moving it off his head.
5. Reward him appropriately when he does this. Repeat step 4 until the child performs independently.

Task Evaluation

1. How long did it take the child to associate the command with the action?

Materials and Equipment

Chair appropriate to child's size
Chair that enables instructor to be at eye level with child
Polo shirt larger than what the child would normally wear but not so large that it just rolls into place

Instructional Objective

To have child remove shirt when it is placed at eye level position.

Readiness

Grasp.
Directs arm movements.
Directs hand movements.

Procedure

1. Place child in a sitting position.
2. Place shirt at eye level on child's head.
3. Give child the command, (name), take your shirt off!
4. Hand over hand, move the child's hands to the bottom of his shirt which will be hanging around his shoulders. Aid him in gathering the shirt into his hands and move it to eye level. He then has to pull the gathered shirt up and over his head.
5. Repeat step 4 until child performs himself.

Task Evaluation

1. Did the child experience much difficulty in gathering the shirt?
2. Did the child move the shirt up and over his head smoothly or did he have to pry at it to get it off?

Materials and Equipment

Chair appropriate to child's size
Chair that enables instructor to be at eye level with child
Polo shirt larger than what the child would normally wear but not so large that it just rolls into place

Instructional Objective

To have child remove shirt when it is placed around his neck.

Readiness

Grasp.
Directed arm movements.
Directed hand movements.

Procedure

1. Place child in a sitting position.
2. Place the shirt around the child's neck.
3. Give the command, (name), take your shirt off!

4. In a hand over hand method, direct the child's hands to the shirt, aid him in gathering the bottom of shirt into his hands. When he has the shirt in his hands, help him pull it up over his face and off.

5. Repeat step 4 until the child can complete the process independently.

Task Evaluation

1. Did the child exhibit any fear of bringing the shirt over his face?

2. Did the child move the shirt over his head easily with a steady movement or did he have to pry to get it off?

Materials and Equipment

Chair appropriate to child's size
Chair that enables instructor to be at eye level with child
Polo shirt larger than what the child would normally wear but
not so large that it just rolls into place

Instructional Objective

To have child remove shirt by releasing one arm from armhole position.

Readiness

Grasp.
Directs arm movements.
Directs hand movements.

Procedure

1. Place the child in a sitting position.

2. Put the shirt over his head and around his neck placing one arm in the arm hole.

3. Give him the command, (name), take off your shirt!

4. The arm and hand should be free from the armhole.

5. Aiding the child in a hand over hand method, gather shirt from under arm position. Pull shirt away from body while bending arm at elbow. Release arm by lowering it through armhole (Fig. 34).

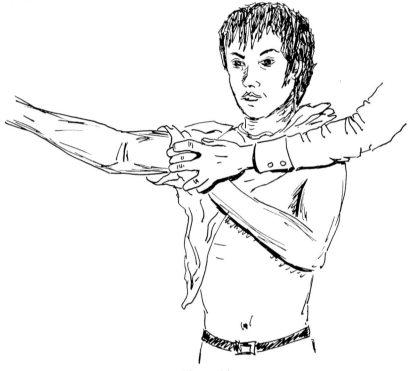

Figure 34

6. He should then independently pull the shirt up and over his head with both hands.

7. The child should practice step 5 until he is self-sufficient.

Task Evaluation

1. Did the child realize that he had to pull the shirt out and away from his body to pull his arm out of the sleeve?

2. Was the child able to hold the shirt out long enough to remove his arm?

Materials and Equipment

Chair appropriate to child's size

Chair that enables instructor to be at eye level with child

Polo shirt larger than what the child would normally wear but not so large that it just rolls into place

Instructional Objective

To have child remove shirt by releasing both arms from armhole position.

Readiness

Grasp.
Directs arm movements.
Directs hand movements.

Procedure

1. Place the child in a sitting position.
2. Put the shirt over his head and around his head and both arms in the armholes, the bottom of the shirt should be at the armpits.
3. Give him command, (name), take off your shirt!
4. Gather shirt from under arm position. Pull shirt away from body while bending elbow. Release arm by lowering it through armhole.
5. Repeat same procedure with opposite arm.
6. He should then proceed to pull the shirt up and over his head.
7. The child should be drilled until he can independently remove the shirt when it is positioned under the armpits.

Task Evaluation

1. Did the child bind himself in the shirt when trying to release his arm?
2. Was he able to hold the shirt out until he released his arm?

Material and Equipment

Chair appropriate to child's size
Chair that enables instructor to be at eye level with child

Polo shirt larger than what the child would normally wear but not so large that it just rolls into place

Instructional Objective

To have child remove shirt from mid-stomach position.

Readiness

Grasp.
Directs arm movements.
Directs hand movements.

Procedure

1. Place the child in a sitting position.
2. Place shirt over head and arms in armholes and down to mid-stomach.
3. Give him command, (name), take off your shirt!
4. In a hand over hand method, gather shirt from mid-stomach and raise to underarm position.
5. Pull shirt away from body while bending elbow. Release arm by lowering it through armhole.
6. The child should practice until he can perform independently as soon as the command is given.

Task Evaluation

1. Did the child exhibit any difficulty in bringing the shirt to the underarm area?
2. Did he easily move from bringing the shirt up to a motion of pulling it out?

Materials and Equipment

Chair appropriate to child's size
Chair that enables instructor to be at eye level with child
Polo shirt larger than what the child would normally wear but not so large that it just rolls into place

Instructional Objective

To have child remove shirt independently.

Readiness

Grasp.
Directs arm movements.
Directs hand movements.

Procedure

1. Place child in a sitting position.
2. Put shirt completely on the child.
3. Give him the command, (name), take off your shirt!
4. In a hand over hand method, gather shirt from completed dress and raise to underarm position.
5. Pull shirt away from body while bending elbow. Release arm by lowering it through armhole.
6. Step 4 should be repeated until the child is consistently successful.

Task Evaluation

1. Did the child experience any difficulty in bringing the shirt up to the underarm area?
2. How long did it take for him to associate the command with the action?

Materials and Equipment

Chair appropriate to child's size
Chair that enables instructor to be at eye level with child
Polo shirt larger than what the child would normally wear but
   not so large that it just rolls into place

Instructional Objective

To have child pull shirt down from mid-stomach position.

Readiness

Grasp.
Begins to direct arm movements.

Procedure

1. Place child in a sitting position.
2. Give him the command, (name), put your shirt on!
3. Place his hands on the bottom of his shirt which is at mid-stomach position.
4. With assistance, have the child pull the shirt into position.
5. This should be repeated until the child is consistently successful.
6. The command should be worded the same way every time and the child's name should be stated.

Task Evaluation

1. Was child able to grasp bottom of shirt?
2. How long did it take for the child to associate the command with the pulling down of his shirt?

Materials and Equipment

Chair appropriate to child's size
Chair that allows instructor to be at approximate eye level with child
Polo shirt larger than what the child might wear but not so large that it just falls down into place

Instructional Objective

To have child pull shirt down from underarm position.

Readiness

Grasp.
Directs arm movements.

Procedure

1. Place child in a sitting position.
2. Give him the command, (name), put your shirt on!
3. Place his hands on the bottom of his shirt which is at the underarm position.
4. Direct his hands downward to position shirt properly.
5. Guide child's hands to shirt positioned under armpits and pull down.
6. Repeat until child is consistently successful.

Task Evaluation

1. Was child able to grasp bottom of shirt?
2. Could child bring the shirt down without too much difficulty, such as tugging and twisting it?
3. How much practice did the child need to be able to bring his own hands under his armpits?
4. Did it take long for the child to associate the command with the action?

Materials and Equipment

Chair appropriate to child's size
Chair that allows instructor to be at approximately eye level with child
Polo shirt larger than what the child might wear but not so large that it falls into place

Instructional Objective

To have child put one arm in armhole and pull shirt down into position.

Readiness

Grasp.
Directs arm movements.
Directs hand movements.

Procedure

1. Place child in a sitting position.
2. Give him the command, (name), put your shirt on!
3. The shirt should be over the child's head and in position around the neck. One arm should be through the armhole, while the arm is released from the armhole.
4. Assisting the child, have him bend his elbow and move his hand under the shirt and through the armhole and pull down.
5. This should be repeated until the child can manipulate his own hand and arm through the armhole.
6. Remember to be consistent with the command and use of name.

Task Evaluation

1. Did the child experience difficulty in getting his hand and arm into the proper position to put into armhole?
2. How much practice did the child need before he could bring his own hand through the armhole?

Materials and Equipment

Chair appropriate to child's size
Chair that allows instructor to be at approximately eye level with child
Polo shirt larger than what the child might wear but not so large that it falls into place

Instructional Objective

To have child put both arms in armholes and pull shirt down into place.

Readiness

Grasp.
Directs arm movements.
Directs hand movements.

Procedure

1. Place child in a sitting position.
2. Give him the command, (name), put your shirt on!
3. The shirt should be over the child's head and in the position around the child's neck, both arms should be released from the armholes.
4. With the child's hand holding the bottom of the shirt down and out, have him move his other hand up and through the armhole.
5. In the same manner have the child hold the bottom of the shirt down and out while the child moves his hand and arm up and through the armhole.
6. For steps 4 and 5 the child may need the instructor's hand over hand assistance.
7. When the child puts both arms in the armholes, he should pull the shirt into place.
8. Repeat the process until the child sufficiently goes through the steps himself.

Task Evaluation

1. Did the child experience difficulty in holding the shirt out with one hand while putting the other through the hole?
2. How much practice did the child need before he could perform the task himself?

Materials and Equipment

Chair appropriate to child's size
Chair that allows instructor to be at approximately eye level with child
Polo shirt larger than what the child might wear but not so large that it falls into place

Instructional Objective

To have child put shirt on from eye level position.

Readiness

Grasp.
Directs arm movements.
Directs hand movements.

Procedure

1. Place child in a sitting position.
2. Give him the command, (name), put your shirt on!
3. The shirt should be just over the head at eye level, both arms released from the armholes.
4. Using a hand over hand method, the child should be aided in pulling the shirt down over the face by placing his hands on the bottom of the shirt to bring it down to the neck.
5. He should then proceed in putting his arms through the armholes and bringing the shirt into place.

Task Evaluation

1. Was the child frightened when shirt was over eyes?
2. Did it take much assistance before the child could perform the task himself?

Materials and Equipment

Chair appropriate to child's size
Chair that allows instructor to be at approximately eye level with child
Polo shirt larger than what the child might wear but not so large that it falls into place

Instructional Objective

To have child put on shirt independently.

Readiness

Grasp.
Directs arm movements.

Directs hand movements.

Knowledge of procedure to follow in placing the shirt over head accurately.

Procedure

1. Place child in a sitting position.
2. Give him the command, (name), put your shirt on!
3. Hand him the shirt showing him the open end. Assist the child by holding his hands in a hand over hand method.
4. His hands should be on the bottom of the shirt holding both sides. The open end of the shirt should be moved to the head and placed over it.
5. Independently, the child should then proceed to pull the shirt down over his face, put his arms in the armholes and pull the shirt into position.
6. The above should be repeated until the child is consistently successful.

Task Evaluation

1. Did the child know to bring the open end of the shirt to the top of his head?
2. Did the child display trouble in putting the shirt over his head?

Materials and Equipment

Chair appropriate to child's size

Chair that allows instructor to be at approximately eye level with child

Polo shirt larger than what the child might wear but not so large that it falls into place

Instructional Objective

To have child successfully take shoes off when only tips of toes are in shoes.

Readiness

Grasp.
Directs foot movements.
Directs leg movements.

Procedure

1. Seat child on chair.
2. Sit on chair.
3. Take shoe almost entirely off child's foot leaving only tips of toes in shoes.
4. Give him the command, (name), take your shoes off!
5. Direct the child to lift his foot up and out of shoe.
6. If necessary grasp child's foot at ankle and assist in lifting up and out of shoe.
7. Repeat steps 4, 5 and 6 until child is consistently successful.

Task Evaluation

1. Did child lift his foot out of shoe in a steady motion?
2. How long did he need the instructor's assistance in lifting his foot out of the shoe?
3. How long did it take until the child was consistently successful?

Materials and Equipment

Chair appropriate to child's size
Chair for instructor that brings him to eye level with child
One size larger shoes

Instructional Objective

To have child take shoe off when only heel of foot is released from shoe.

Readiness

Grasp.
Directs leg movements.
Directs foot movements.

Procedure

1. Seat child on chair.
2. Sit on chair.
3. Release heel and back part of child's foot from shoe (Fig. 35).

Figure 35

4. Give child the command, (name), take off your shoes!
5. Direct child to slide his foot back toward the heel of his shoe until his toes are exposed.
6. If necessary, grasp child's foot at the ankle and pull back.
7. Instruct child to lift foot up and out of shoe.
8. Repeat steps 4 through 7 until child is consistently successful.

Task Evaluation

1. Did child readily learn that he had to slide his foot back before lifting foot out of shoe?
2. How long did he need the assistance in sliding his foot back?
3. How long did it take until the child was consistently successful?

Materials and Equipment

Chair appropriate for child's size
Chair that brings instructor to eye level with child
One size larger shoes

Instructional Objective

To have child take off shoe independently.

Readiness

Grasp.
Directs foot movements.
Directs leg movements.

Procedure

1. Seat child on chair.
2. Sit on chair.
3. Place shoe entirely on child's foot.
4. Give child the command, (name), take off your shoe!
5. Instruct child to lift heel up and out of shoe.
6. He should then slide the rest of his foot back toward the heel of the shoe and lift the foot out of the shoe.
7. If necessary, guide the child's foot in the proper manner by grasping the ankle until he understands proper movements and is consistently successful.

Task Evaluation

1. Did child quickly learn that he had to lift his heel out of the shoe before he could release the rest of his foot?
2. Did child readily learn that he had to slide his foot back before lifting foot out of shoe?
3. How long did he need the assistance in sliding his foot back?

4. How long did it take until the child was consistently successful?

Materials and Equipment

Chair appropriate for child's size
Chair for instructor that brings him to eye level with child
One size larger shoes

Instructional Objective

To have child put shoe on when foot is in shoe, but heel is not in proper position.

Readiness

Grasp.
Directs foot movements.
Directs leg movements.

Procedure

1. Seat child on chair.
2. Sit on chair.
3. Place shoe on child's foot.
4. Give child the command, (name), put your shoe on!
5. Direct the child to push his heel down into proper position.
6. If necessary grasp child's ankle and exert a downward force until the child realizes the sensation of pushing down and having his foot go into proper position.
7. Repeat steps 4, 5 and 6 until child is consistently successful.

Task Evaluation

1. Did child push his heel into the shoe in a smooth motion or did he rock the shoe from side to side to get the heel into place?
2. How long did it take until he learned that he had to push his heel down to position his foot correctly in the shoe?

3. How long did it take until the child was consistently successful?

Materials and Equipment

Chair appropriate to child's size
Chair for instructor that brings him to eye level with child
One size larger shoes

Instructional Objective

To have child put shoe on when toes and middle foot are in shoe but heel is completely out of shoe.

Readiness

Grasp.
Directs foot movements.
Directs leg movements.

Procedure

1. Seat child on chair.
2. Sit on chair.
3. Place shoe on child's foot leaving heel out of shoe.
4. Give child the command, (name), put your shoe on!
5. Direct child to push foot forward so there is enough room in back of shoe for heel.
6. If necessary, grasp child's foot at ankle and push forward in shoe.
7. Instruct child to push heel down into proper position.
8. Repeat steps 4 through 7 until the child is consistently successful.

Task Evaluation

1. By going through the motion of pushing the child's foot forward in the shoe, did he quickly learn that he had to move his toes up in the shoe to make room for his heel?

2. Did child push his heel down into the shoe in a smooth motion, or did he rock the shoe from side to side to get his heel in place?

3. How long did it take until he learned that he had to push his heel down to position his foot correctly in the shoe?

4. How long did it take until the child was consistently successful?

Materials and Equipment

Chair appropriate to child's size
Chair for adult that brings him to eye level with child
One size larger shoes

Instructional Objective

To have child successfully put on shoes when only tips of toes are in shoe.

Readiness

Grasp.
Directs foot movements.
Directs leg movements.

Procedure

1. Seat child on chair.

2. Sit on chair.

3. Place shoe on child's foot; just child's toes should be in shoe.

4. Give child the command, (name), put your shoe on!

5. Instruct child to push foot forward until there is room in back of shoe for heel.

6. If necessary, grasp the child's foot at ankle and push forward in shoe.

7. Instruct child to push heel down into proper position.

8. Repeat steps 4 through 7 until the child is consistently successful.

Task Evaluation

1. By going through the motion of pushing the child's foot forward in the shoe, did he learn that he had to move his toes up in the shoe to make room for his heel?
2. Did child push his heel down into the shoe in a smooth motion, or did he rock the shoe from side to side to get his heel in place?
3. How long did it take until he learned that he had to push his heel down to position his foot correctly in the shoe?
4. How long did it take until the child was consistently successful?

Materials and Equipment

Chair appropriate to child's size
Chair for adult that brings him to eye level with child
One size larger shoes

Instructional Objective

To have child successfully put on shoes independently.

Readiness

Grasp.
Directs foot movements.
Directs leg movements.

Procedure

1. Seat child on chair.
2. Sit on chair.
3. Place shoe on floor directly in front of foot.
4. Give child the command, (name), put on your shoe!

5. Direct child to lift leg and point toes into shoes.

6. If necessary, guide child's foot into shoe by grasping at ankle.

7. Direct child to push foot forward so there is enough room in back of shoe for heel.

8. Instruct child to push heel down into proper position.

9. Repeat steps 4 through 8 until the child is consistently successful.

Task Evaluation

1. Was the child able to direct foot into shoe or did he push shoe over trying to get his foot in?

2. How long did it take until the child smoothly moved his foot up into the tip of the shoe?

3. Did child push his heel down into the shoe in a smooth motion, or did he rock the shoe from side to side to get his heel in place?

4. How long did it take until the child was consistently successful?

Materials and Equipment

Chair appropriate to child's size
Chair for instructor that brings him to eye level with child
One size larger shoes

Instructional Objective

To have child successfully take hat off when hat is just on top of head.

Readiness

Grasp with both hands.
Directs arm movements.
Directs hand movements.

Procedure

1. Stand child in front of mirror.
2. Place hat on top of head.
3. Give child the command, (name), take your hat off!
4. Direct child to move his hand to top of hat, grasp hat and pull off; use hand over hand method if necessary.
5. Repeat steps 3 and 4 until child is consistently successful.

Task Evaluation

1. Was child able to grasp top of hat and pull off?
2. Did he use the mirror for assistance in seeing top of hat?
3. Were his motions steady?
4. How long did it take until the child was consistently successful?

Materials and Equipment

Stretch tassel hat

Instructional Objective

To have child successfully take hat off when hat is pulled half way into position.

Readiness

Grasps with both hands.
Directs arm movements.
Directs hand movements.

Procedure

1. Stand child in front of mirror.
2. Place hat half way on head.
3. Give child the command, (name), take off your hat!
4. Direct child to place both hands at the side edges of hat and

push up to top of head. Use hand over hand method of instruction if necessary.

5. Direct child to move his hand to top of head, grasp hat and pull off. Use hand over hand method if necessary.

6. Repeat steps 3, 4 and 5 until child is consistently successful.

Task Evaluation

1. Was child able to grasp top of hat and pull off?
2. Was child able to grasp with both hands and push hat off?
3. Did he use the mirror for assistance in seeing the top of the hat?
4. Were his motions steady?
5. How long did it take before the child was consistently successful?

Materials and Equipment

Stretch tassel hat

Instructional Objective

To have child successfully take hat off independently.

Readiness

Grasps with both hands.
Directs arm movements.
Directs hand movements.

Procedure

1. Stand child in front of mirror.
2. Place hat entirely on head.
3. Give child the command, (name), take off your hat!
4. Direct child to place both hands at the side edges of the hat and push up to top of head.
5. Direct child to move his hand to top of head, grasp hat and pull off.
6. Repeat steps 3, 4 and 5 until child is consistently successful.

Task Evaluation

1. Was child able to grasp with both hands and push hat off?
2. Was child able to grasp top of hat and pull off?
3. Did he use the mirror for assistance in seeing top of hat?
4. Were his motions steady?
5. How long did it take until the child was consistently successful?

Materials and Equipment

Stretch tassel hat

Instructional Objective

To have child successfully put hat on when it is half way placed on his head.

Readiness

Grasp with both hands.
Directs arm movements.
Directs hand movements.

Procedure

1. Stand child in front of mirror.
2. Put hat half way on head.
3. Give child the command, (name), put your hat on!
4. Direct him to bring both hands to his head and grasp each side of the hat and pull down into position. Use hand over hand method of necessary.
5. Repeat steps 3 and 4 until the child is consistently successful.

Task Evaluation

1. Did child grasp with both hands at the same time?
2. Were his motions steady?

3. How long did it take until the child was consistently successful?

Materials and Equipment

Stretch tassel hat

Instructional Objective

To have child successfully put hat on when it is on top of head.

Readiness

Grasp with both hands.
Directs arm movements.
Directs hand movements.

Procedure

1. Stand child in front of mirror.
2. Put hat just on top of head.
3. Give child the command, (name), put your hat on!
4. Direct him to bring both hands to his head and grasp each side of the hat and pull down into position. Use hand over hand method if necessary.
5. Repeat steps 3 and 4 until the child is consistently successful.

Task Evaluation

1. Did child grasp with both hands at the same time?
2. Were his motions steady?
3. How long did it take until he was consistently successful?

Materials and Equipment

Stretch tassel hat

Instructional Objective

To have child successfully put on hat independently.

Readiness

Grasp with both hands.
Directs arm movements.
Directs hand movements.

Procedure

1. Stand child in front of mirror.
2. Give child the command, (name), put your hat on!
3. Hand the child the hat showing him that by grasping each side at the edge he can hold hat open so as to be able to place it on top of his head.
4. Direct child to move his hands holding open that hat to the top of his head and placing the hat on top of head.
5. Direct him to pull the hat down into position.
6. Repeat steps 2 through 5 until child is consistently successful.

Task Evaluation

1. Did child grasp with both hands?
2. Were his motions steady?
3. Was he able to hold hat open to be able to put it on his head?
4. Was he able to bring the hat up and place on top of his head?
5. How long did it take until the child was consistently successful?

Materials and Equipment

Stretch tassel hat

Instructional Objective

To have child take off mitten when thumb is released and mitten is only partially on four fingers.

Readiness

Grasp.
Directs arm movements.
Directs hand movements.

Procedure

1. Seat child on chair.
2. Sit on chair.
3. Place mitten on child having thumb out of thumb slot and mitten just partially on child's four fingers. Other hand should be free.
4. Give child the command, (name), take your mitten off!
5. Instruct him to grasp end of mitten with hand and pull off. Use a hand over hand method if necessary.
6. Repeat steps 3, 4 and 5 until child is consistently successful.

Task Evaluation

1. Did child grasp end of mitten firmly enough with hand to pull off in a steady motion?

Materials and Equipment

Stretch mitten half size larger than what the child would normally wear.

Instructional Objective

To have child take mitten off when mitten is only half way over thumb and four fingers are in proper position.

Readiness

Grasp.
Directs arm movements.
Directs hand movements.

Procedure

1. Seat child on chair.
2. Sit on chair.
3. Place mitten half way on child's hand leaving other hand free.
4. Give child the command, (name), take your mitten off!
5. Instruct him to grasp end of mitten with hand and pull off. Use a hand over hand method if necessary.
6. Repeat steps 3, 4 and 5 until child is consistently successful.

Task Evaluation

1. Did child grasp end of mitten firmly enough with hand to pull off in a steady motion?

Materials and Equipment

Stretch mitten half size larger than what the child would normally wear

Instructional Objective

To have child take mitten off independently.

Readiness

Grasp.
Directs arm movements.
Directs hand movements.

Procedure

1. Seat child on chair.
2. Sit on chair.
3. Place mitten entirely on child's hand.
4. Give child the command, (name), take off your mitten!
5. Instruct him to grasp end of mitten with hand and pull off.
6. Repeat steps 3, 4 and 5 until child is consistently successful.

Task Evaluation

1. Did child grasp end of mitten firmly enough with hand to pull off in a steady motion?

Materials and Equipment

Stretch mitten half size larger than what the child would normally wear

Instructional Objective

To have child put mitten on when thumb and four fingers are positioned properly and mitten is half way on.

Readiness

Grasp.
Pincer grasp.
Directs arm movements.
Directs hand movements.

Procedure

1. Sit child on chair.
2. Sit on chair.
3. Place mitten half way on child's hand leaving other hand free with thumb and four fingers in proper position.
4. Give child the command, (name), put your mitten on!
5. Direct child to pincer grasp end of mitten with hand and pull into position. Use hand over hand method if necessary.
6. Repeat steps 4, 5 and 6 until child is consistently successful.

Task Evaluation

1. Was child able to grasp end of mitten and pull into place?
2. Were his pulling motions steady?
3. How long did it take until the child could follow through independently?

Materials and Equipment

Knit mitten somewhat larger than what the child would normally wear

Instructional Objective

To have child put mitten on when thumb and four fingers are positioned properly, when mitten is a quarter of the way on.

Readiness

Grasp.
Pincer grasp.
Directs arm movements.
Directs hand movements.

Procedure

1. Seat child on chair.
2. Sit on chair.
3. Place mitten a quarter of the way on child's hand leaving other hand free with thumb and four fingers in proper position.
4. Give child the command, (name), put your mitten on!
5. Direct child to pincer grasp end of mitten with hand and pull into position; use hand over hand method if necessary (Fig. 36).
6. Repeat steps 4, 5 and 6 until child is consistently successful.

Task Evaluation

1. Was child able to grasp end of mitten and pull into place?
2. Were his pulling motions steady?
3. How long did it take until the child was consistently successful?

Figure 36

Materials and Equipment

Knit mittens somewhat larger than what the child would normally wear

Instructional Objective

To have child put mitten on independently.

Readiness

Grasp.
Pincer grasp.
Directs arm movements.
Directs hand movements.

Procedure

1. Seat child on chair.
2. Sit on chair.
3. Hand mitten to child.
4. Give child the command, (name), put your mitten on!
5. Direct him to pincer grasp mitten by one end with hand and hold so that end is open wide enough for him to slip his other hand in.
6. Instruct him to put other hand in mitten and slipping thumb into place, pull mitten into place.

Task Evaluation

1. Was child able to hold open end of mitten sufficiently to put his hand in?
2. Did he hold mitten securely enough that he didn't push it out of his hand when he was putting his other hand into the mitten?
3. Was child able to grasp end of mitten and pull into place?
4. Were his pulling motions steady?
5. How long did it take until he was consistently successful?

Materials and Equipment

Knit mitten somewhat larger than what the child would normally wear

Instructional Objective

To have child successfully take coat off when one hand and arm are released from sleeve and coat is on shoulder.

Readiness

Grasp.
Directs arm movements.
Directs hand movements.

Procedure

1. Stand child in front of mirror.
2. Release child's arm, but leave coat on shoulder.
3. Give child the command, (name), take off your coat!
4. Instruct child to push coat from shoulder with hand. If necessary, use hand over hand method.
5. Direct him to grasp end of sleeve with hand.
6. He should then pull coat down and off arm.
7. Repeat steps 3 through 6 until the child is consistently successful.

Task Evaluation

1. Was child able to move his arm up to push coat off shoulder?
2. Did he grasp the sleeve firmly enough to pull the coat off?
3. How long did it take until the child was consistently successful?

Materials and Equipment

Large full length mirror
Coat one size larger than what the child would normally wear

Instructional Objective

To have child take off coat independently.

Readiness

Grasp.
Directs arm movements.
Directs hand movements.

Procedure

1. Stand child in front of mirror.
2. Place coat on child.
3. Give child the command, (name), take off your coat!
4. Instruct child to grasp front of coat.
5. He should open the coat wide in order to release his shoulder.
6. Direct him to lift his arm up and out of the sleeve, he may have to shake his arm slightly to remove his sleeve. Aid him if necessary by grasping his arm at elbow.
7. Guide him to grasp end of sleeve with hand.
8. He should then pull coat down and off arm.
9. Repeat steps 3 through 8 until the child is consistently successful.

Task Evaluation

1. Did child grasp side of coat firmly with hand?
2. Did he pull coat to side smoothly to release shoulder?
3. Was he able to release his arm from armhole independently, shaking his arm to help the sleeve slide off?
4. Did he grasp the sleeve firmly enough to pull the coat off?
5. How long did it take until the child was consistently successful?

Materials and Equipment

Large full length mirror
Coat one size larger than what the child would normally wear

Instructional Objective

To have child put on coat when one arm is released.

Readiness

Grasp.
Directs arm movements.
Directs hand movements.

Procedure

1. Stand child in front of mirror.
2. Place coat on one arm and shoulder leaving other arm free from coat.
3. Give child the command, (name), put on your coat!
4. Direct child to move his arm around to his back and locate the armhole (Fig. 37).
5. If necessary, guide his hand to the armhole.
6. Instruct him to put his hand into the armhole and slide his arm down through the sleeve.
7. He should then move his elbow up to lift the coat to his shoulders.
8. If necessary, aid the child in getting the coat on to his shoulders by manipulating his elbow into the correct positions.
9. Repeat steps 3 through 8 until the child is consistently successful.

Task Evaluation

1. Was child able to find armhole by feeling for it rather than seeing it?
2. Was he able to put his arm through sleeve when the coat was toward his back?
3. Did child move arm down through sleeve of coat?
4. Did he manipulate his elbow and shoulder in the correct way to bring the coat up to his shoulders?
5. How long did he need the assistance before he was consistently successful?

Figure 37

Materials and Equipment

Large full length mirror
Coat one size larger than what the child would normally wear

Instructional Objective

To have child successfully put coat on by pushing arm through armhole when coat is positioned.

Readiness

Grasp.
Directs arm movements.
Directs hand movements.

Procedure

1. Stand child in front of mirror.
2. Place coat on child with one arm partially in armhole.
3. Give child the command, (name), put on your coat!
4. Instruct child to push hand and arm down through armhole and into proper position.
5. If necessary, aid child by grasping elbow and pushing arm down into position.
6. Repeat steps 3, 4 and 5 until the child is consistently successful.

Task Evaluation

1. Did child move arm down through sleeve of coat?
2. How long did he need the instructors assistance in moving his arm down the sleeve?

Materials and Equipment

One large full length mirror
Coat one size larger than what the child would normally wear

Instructional Objective

To have child successfully put coat on when coat is held.

Readiness

Grasp.
Pincer grasp.

Directs arm movements.
Directs hand movements.

Procedure

1. Stand child in front of mirror.
2. Hold coat making armhole visible.
3. Give child the command, (name), put on your coat!
4. Instruct child to bring arm up and place through sleeve while instructor is holding coat.
5. When child has arm through sleeve, let go of coat and let him do the rest himself.
6. He should bring his other arm around and with his hand locate armhole, slide arm through sleeve into proper position.
7. He should then lift his elbow up and out to bring the coat to his shoulder.
8. Repeat steps 3 through 7 until the child is consistently successful.

Task Evaluation

1. Did child place arm in armhole and sleeve easily?
2. Was child able to find armhole by feeling for it rather than seeing it?
3. Did child move arm down through sleeve of coat?
4. Did he manipulate his elbow and shoulder in the correct way to bring the coat up to his shoulders?
5. How long did it take until the child was consistently successful?

Materials and Equipment

Full length mirror
Coat one size larger than what the child would normally wear

Instructional Objective

To have child put coat on independently.

Readiness

Grasp.
Directs arm movements.
Directs hand movements.

Procedure

1. Stand child in front of full length mirror.
2. Hand child coat. It should be held above armhole.
3. Give child the command, (name), put on your coat!
4. Instruct child to bring arm up and place it through sleeve while sliding the coat up to the shoulder with the other hand.
5. When arm is in proper position and coat is on one shoulder, he should bring his other arm around and with his hand locate armhole and slide arm through sleeve into proper position.
6. He should then lift his elbow up and out to bring the coat to his shoulder.
7. Repeat steps 3 through 6 until the child is consistently successful.

Task Evaluation

1. Was child able to hold coat firmly with one hand while placing the other arm through sleeve?
2. Did he correctly bring coat up to shoulder with hand?
3. Was child able to find armhole by feeling for it rather than seeing it?
4. Did child move arm down through sleeve of coat smoothly?
5. Did he manipulate his elbow and shoulder in the correct way to bring the coat up to his shoulder?
6. How long did it take until the child was consistently successful?

Materials and Equipment

Full length mirror
Coat one size larger than what the child would normally wear

Instructional Objective

To have child successfully unsnap pants when hands are positioned properly.

Readiness

Pincer grasp.
Directs arm movements.
Directs hand movements.
Can pull with both hands simultaneously while in pincer grasp position.

Procedure

1. Seat child on chair.
2. Sit on chair.
3. Place pants that snap at waist on child. Snap should be fastened.
4. Give child the command, (name), unsnap your pants!
5. Position child's hand on left side of pants with a pincer grasp. Thumb on inside and index finger on the outside. Right hand should be positioned on the right side of the pants, thumb on inside and index finger on the outside on top of snap. Use hand over hand method if necessary.
6. Direct the child to pull the right side of the pants with right hand toward him while pulling left side of pants with left hand away from him. Use hand over hand method if necessary.
7. Repeat steps 4, 5 and 6 until child is consistently successful.

Task Evaluation

1. Did child maintain good grasp on pants with both hands?
2. Was child able to pull snaps apart with both hands simultaneously?
3. Were his motions steady?
4. How long did it take until the child was consistently successful?

Materials and Equipment

Chair appropriate for child's size

Chair for adult that brings him to eye level with child
Pants with large snap at waist band

Instructional Objective

To have child successfully unsnap pants independently.

Readiness

Pincer grasp.
Directs hand movements.
Directs arm movements.
Can pull with both hands simultaneously while in pincer grasp position.

Procedure

1. Seat child on chair.
2. Sit on chair.
3. Place pants with snaps on child. Snap should be fastened.
4. Give child the command, (name), unsnap your pants!
5. Direct child to position right hand in a pincer grasp on right side of pants and left hand in same manner on left side of pants.
6. He should then pull the right side of the pants with his right hand toward him by pulling the left side of the pants with the left hand away from him.
7. Repeat steps 4, 5 and 6 until the child is consistently successful.

Task Evaluation

1. Did child maintain good grasp on pants with both hands?
2. Was child able to pull snaps on pants apart with both hands simultaneously?
3. Were motions steady?
4. Did child position his own hands accurately?
5. How long did it take until the child was consistently successful?

Materials and Equipment

Chair appropriate for child's size
Chair for adult that brings him to eye level with child
Pants with large snap at waist band

Instructional Objective

To have child successfully snap pants when top of snap is positioned on bottom, but not fastened.

Readiness

Pincer grasp.
Directs arm movements.
Directs hand movements.
Can exert force with thumb and index finger.

Procedure

1. Seat child on chair.
2. Sit on chair.
3. Place pants that snap at waist band on child. Snap should be somewhat large.
4. The snap should be unfastened, but top should be sitting on bottom.
5. Give child the command, (name), snap your pants!
6. Instruct right-handed child to pincer grasp the left side of the pants near the snap with the left hand. Left thumb should be directly on the snap of the inside of the pants and pincer grasp. The right side of the pants should be grasped with the right hand; the right index finger should be on top of the snap on the inside of the pants.
7. Direct the child to hold left thumb and right hand steady while pushing the snap together by exerting force with the left index finger. Use hand over hand method if necessary.
8. Repeat steps 5, 6 and 7 until the child is consistently successful.

Task Evaluation

1. Did child maintain good pincer grasp on pants with both hands?
2. Was child able to exert enough force with left index finger to fasten snap?
3. How long did it take until the child was consistently successful?

Materials and Equipment

Chair appropriate for child's size
Chair for adult that brings him to eye level with the child
Pants with somewhat large snap at waist band

Instructional Objective

To have child successfully snap pants independently.

Readiness

Pincer grasp.
Directs arm movements.
Directs hand movements.
Can exert force with thumb and index finger.

Procedure

1. Seat child on chair.
2. Sit on chair.
3. Place pants that snap at waist band on child. Snap should be somewhat large.
4. Pants should be unfastened.
5. Give child the command, (name), snap your pants!
6. Command child to pincer grasp the left side of the pants near the snap with the left hand. Left thumb should be directly on the snap on the inside of the pants and pincer grasp the right side of the pants with right hand; right index finger should be on top of the snap in the inside of the pants (Fig. 38).

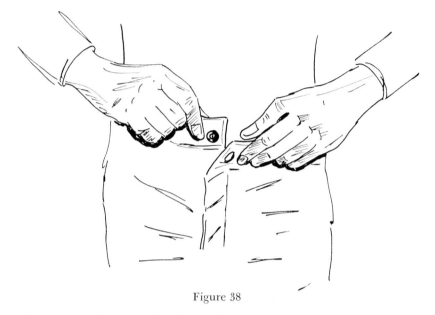

Figure 38

7. Direct the right-handed child to hold right side of pants while bringing left side of pants over to and on top of snap.

8. Instruct him to hold right thumb and right hand steady while pushing snap together by exerting force with left index finger.

9. Repeat steps 5 through 8 until the child is consistently successful.

Task Evaluation

1. Did child maintain good pincer grasp on pants with both hands?

2. Was child able to exert enough force with left index finger to fasten snap?

3. Did child accurately bring top and bottom of snap together?

4. How long did it take until the child was consistently successful?

Materials and Equipment

Chair appropriate to child's size
Chair for adult that brings him to eye level with child
Pants with large snap at waist band

Instructional Objective

To have child unzip coat when zipper is three-fourths of the way down.

Readiness

Grasp.
Pincer grasp.
Directs arm movements.
Directs hand movements.

Procedure

1. Place jacket with large zipper on child.
2. Unzip jacket three-fourths of the way.
3. Give child the command, (name), unzip your jacket!
4. Direct child to pincer grasp with hand tab of zipper. His other hand should be grasping the coat near the zipper holding it steady. Use a hand over hand method if necessary.
5. Instruct the child to pull tab down toward waist and then lift end of zipper out of slot with hand. Use hand over hand method of instruction if necessary.
6. Repeat steps 3, 4 and 5 until the child is consistently successful.

Task Evaluation

1. Was child able to pincer grasp zipper tab and pull down while maintaining grasp?
2. Did he hold side of coat steady with the other hand?
3. Were his motions steady?
4. How long did it take until the child was consistently successful?

Materials and Equipment

Coat with large zipper and large tab

Instructional Objective

To have child successfully unzip coat when zipper is one-half the way down.

Readiness

Grasp.
Pincer grasp.
Directs arm movements.
Directs hand movements.

Procedure

1. Place jacket with large zipper on child.
2. Unzip jacket one-half of the way.
3. Give child the command, (name), unzip your jacket!
4. Direct child to pincer grasp with hand tab of zipper. His other hand should be grasping the coat near the zipper holding it steady. Use a hand over hand method of instruction if necessary.
5. Instruct child to pull tab down toward waist and then lift end of zipper out of slot with hand. Use hand over hand method of instruction if necessary.
6. Repeat steps 3, 4 and 5 until child is consistently successful.

Task Evaluation

1. Was child able to pincer grasp tab and pull down while maintaining grasp?
2. Did he hold side of coat steady with other hand?
3. Were his motions steady?
4. How long did it take until the child was consistently successful?

Materials and Equipment

Coat with large zipper and large tab

Instructional Objective

To have child successfully unzip coat independently.

Readiness

Grasp.
Pincer grasp.
Directs arm movements.
Directs hand movements.

Procedure

1. Place jacket with large zipper on child.
2. Leave jacket zipped up.
3. Give child the command, (name), unzip your jacket!
4. Direct child to pincer grasp tab of zipper. His other hand should be grasping the coat near the zipper holding it steady.
5. Instruct child to pull tab down with hand while the other is holding the coat steady.
6. While his hand is grasping the zipper tab steady, the child with the other hand should pick up the side of the zipper that the straight end is on and lift it out of the zipper slot.
7. Repeat steps 3 through 6 until the child is consistently successful.

Task Evaluation

1. Was child able to pincer grasp zipper tab and pull down while maintaining grasp?
2. Did he hold side of coat steady with other hand?
3. Was the child able to lift the end of the zipper out of the zipper slot easily or did he have to tug to get it out?
4. Were his motions steady?
5. How long did it take until the child was consistently successful?

Materials and Equipment

Coat with large zipper and large tab

Instructional Objective

To have child successfully zip coat when the zipper is three-fourths of the way up.

Readiness

Grasp.
Pincer grasp.
Directs arm movements.
Directs hand movements.

Procedure

1. Place jacket with large zipper on child.
2. Zip the jacket three-fourths of the way up.
3. Give child the command, (name), zip your jacket!
4. Direct child to pincer grasp with hand tab and zipper. His other hand should be grasping the coat near the zipper holding it steady. Use a hand over hand method if necessary.
5. Instruct child to pull tab up toward neck with hand while other is holding coat steady. Use hand over hand method if necessary.
6. Repeat steps 3, 4 and 5 until child is consistently successful.

Task Evaluation

1. Was child able to grasp zipper tab and pull up while maintaining grasp?
2. Did he hold side of coat steady with other hand?

Materials and Equipment

Coat with large zipper and large tab

Instructional Objective

To have child successfully zip coat when the zipper is one-half of the way up.

Readiness

Grasp.
Pincer grasp.
Directs arm movements.
Directs hand movements.

Procedure

1. Place jacket with large zipper on child.
2. Zip the jacket zipper one-half of the way up.
3. Give child the command, (name), zip your coat!
4. Direct child to pincer grasp with hand tab of zipper. His other hand should be grasping the coat near the zipper holding it steady. Use hand over hand method if necessary.
5. Instruct child to pull tab up toward neck with hand while other is holding coat steady. Use a hand over hand method if necessary.
6. Repeat steps 3, 4 and 5 until child is consistently successful.

Task Evaluation

1. Was child able to pincer grasp zipper tab and pull up while maintaining grasp?
2. Did he hold side of coat steady with other hand?
3. Were his motions steady?
4. How long did it take until the child was consistently successful?

Materials and Equipment

Coat with large zipper and large tab

Instructional Objective

To have child successfully zip coat when the zipper is one-fourth of the way up.

Readiness

Grasp.
Pincer grasp.
Directs arm movements.
Directs hand movements.

Procedure

1. Place jacket with large zipper on child.
2. Zip the jacket zipper one-fourth of the way up.
3. Give child the command, (name), zip your coat!
4. Direct child to pincer grasp with hand tab of the zipper; his other hand should be grasping the coat near the zipper holding it steady. Use a hand over hand method of instruction if necessary.
5. Instruct child to pull tab up toward his neck with hand while other is holding coat steady. Use hand over hand method if necessary.
6. Repeat steps 3, 4 and 5 until child is consistently successful.

Task Evaluation

1. Was child able to pincer grasp zipper tab and pull up while maintaining grasp?
2. Did he hold side of coat steady with other hand?
3. Were his motions steady?
4. How long did it take until the child was consistently successful?

Materials and Equipment

Coat with large zipper and large tab

Instructional Objective

To have child successfully zip coat independently.

Readiness

Grasp.
Pincer grasp.
Directs arm movements.
Directs hand movements.

Procedure

1. Place jacket with large zipper on child.
2. Leave zipper unattached.
3. Give child the command, (name), zip your coat!
4. Direct child to hold side of jacket with one hand while he picks up the other side of the jacket with his other hand and places end of zipper in zipper slot.
5. He should then be instructed to grasp tab with hand and side of coat with other hand.
6. Instruct him to pull the tab up to his neck with his hand while holding the coat steady with the other hand.
7. Repeat steps 3 through 6 until child is consistently successful.

Task Evaluation

1. Were child's hand movements coordinated sufficiently to put the end of the zipper into zipper slot?
2. Could he alternate his grasp from grasping one side from the other with thumb and hand?
3. Was child able to pincer grasp zipper tab and pull up while maintaining grasp?
4. Did he hold side of coat steady with other hand?
5. Were his motions straight?
6. How long did it take until the child was consistently successful?

Materials and Equipment

Coat with large zipper and large tab

Instructional Objective

To have child successfully unbutton shirt when button is three-fourths of the way through the buttonhole.

Readiness

Pincer grasp.
Directs arm movements.
Directs hand movements.
Can alternate pincer grasp to left and right hand.

Procedure

1. Seat child on chair.
2. Sit on chair.
3. Place shirt with large buttons on right side of child.
4. Work on middle button with child. This is easily accessible to him.
5. Unbutton the middle button three-fourths of the way, leaving one-fourth of the button in the buttonhole.
6. Give the child the command, (name), unbutton your shirt!
7. Instruct child to grasp both sides of the button in a pincer grasp.
8. He should be directed to push the button with the right hand (in the pincer grasp position) while pulling with the left hand (also in a pincer grasp).
9. Repeat steps 6, 7 and 8 until the child is consistently successful.

Task Evaluation

1. Did child maintain good grasp on button?
2. Could he use both hands in a pincer grasp position at the same time?
3. Were his motions smooth or did he pull and tug to get button through buttonhole?
4. How long did it take until the child was consistently success ful?

Materials and Equipment

Chair appropriate to child's size
Chair for adult that brings him to eye level with child
Shirt with large buttons and buttonholes; buttons should be on
   right side of shirt

Instructional Objective

To have child successfully unbutton shirt when button is one-
half way through buttonhole.

Readiness

Pincer grasp.
Directs arm movements.
Directs hand movements.
Can alternate pincer grasp to left and right hand.

Procedure

1. Seat child on chair.
2. Sit on chair.
3. Place shirt that buttons on right side on child.
4. Work on middle button with child; this is easily accessible
to him.
5. Unbutton the middle button one-half of the way leaving
half of button in the buttonhole.
6. Give the child the command, (name), unbutton your shirt!
7. Instruct child to grasp both sides of the button in the pincer
grasp.
8. He should then be directed to push the button with the
right hand (in a pincer grasp position) while pulling with the
left (also in a pincer grasp position).
9. Repeat steps 6, 7 and 8 until child is consistently successful.

Task Evaluation

1. Did child maintain good grasp on button?

2. Could he use both hands in a pincer grasp position at the same time?

3. Were his motions smooth or did he pull and tug to get the button through?

4. How long did it take before the child was consistently successful?

Materials and Equipment

Chair appropriate to child's size
Chair for adult that brings him to eye level with child
Shirt with large buttons on right side

Instructional Objective

To have child unbutton independently.

Readiness

Pincer grasp.
Directs arm movements.
Directs hand movements.
Can alternate pincer grasp to left and right hand.

Procedure

1. Seat child on chair.

2. Sit on chair.

3. Place shirt with large buttonholes on right side on child.

4. Work on middle button with child; this is easily accessible to him.

5. Leave middle button buttoned.

6. Give the child the command, (name), unbutton your shirt!

7. Instruct child to grasp the button in a pincer grasp with the right hand while grasping left side of the shirt near buttonhole with left hand in a pincer grasp.

8. Direct child to pick up button with left hand and push through buttonhole when button is half of the way through child's shirt. Move right hand to button and pull the rest of the way through using a pincer grasp.

9. Repeat steps 6, 7 and 8 until the child is consistently successful.

Task Evaluation

1. Did child maintain good grasp on button?
2. Could he use both hands in a pincer grasp?
3. Were his motions smooth or did he pull and tug to get button through hole?
4. Did child easily move left hand from grasping shirt to grasping the button to pull through buttonhole?
5. How long did it take before the child was consistently successful?

Materials and Equipment

Chair appropriate for child's size
Chair for adult that brings him to eye level with child
Shirt with large buttons on right side

Instructional Objective

To have child successfully button shirt when button is three-fourths of the way through buttonhole.

Readiness

Pincer grasps.
Directs arm movements.
Directs hand movements.
Can alternate pincer grasp to left and right hand.

Procedure

1. Seat child on chair.
2. Sit on chair.
3. Place shirt with large buttons on right side on child.
4. Work on middle button with child; this is easily accessible to him.

5. Button middle button three-fourths of the way leaving a fourth of the button out of the buttonhole.

6. Give child the command, (name), button your shirt!

7. Instruct child to pincer grasp button with right hand and pincer grasp shirt near buttonhole with left hand.

8. Direct him to push the button through the buttonhole with the right hand. Use hand over hand method if necessary.

9. Repeat steps 5 through 8 until the child is consistently successful.

Task Evaluation

1. Did child maintain good grasp on buttons?

2. Could he use both hands in a pincer grasp position at the same time?

3. Were his motions smooth or did he pull and tug to get buttons through buttonhole?

4. How long did it take before the child was consistently successful?

Materials and Equipment

Chair appropriate for child's size
Chair for adult that brings him to eye level with child
Shirt with somewhat large buttons on right side

Instructional Objective

To have child successfully button shirt when button is one-half way through buttonhole.

Readiness

Pincer grasp.
Directs arm movements.
Directs hand movements.
Can alternate pincer grasp to left and right hand.

Procedure

1. Seat child on chair.
2. Sit on chair.
3. Place shirt with large buttons on right side on child.
4. Work on middle button with child; this is easily accessible to him.
5. Button middle button one-half way.
6. Give child the command, (name), button your shirt!
7. Instruct child to pincer grasp button with right hand and with left hand pincer grasp shirt near buttonhole (Fig. 39).

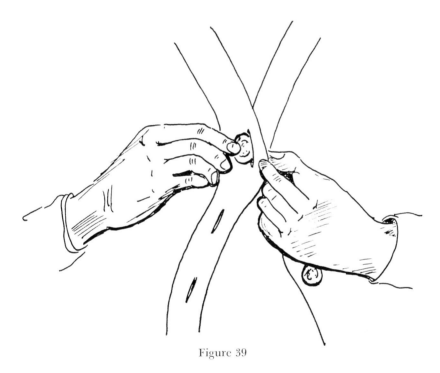

Figure 39

8. Direct him to push the button through the buttonhole with the right hand. Use hand over hand method if necessary.
9. Repeat steps 5 through 8 until the child is consistently successful.

Task Evaluation

1. Did child maintain good grasp on buttons?
2. Could he use both hands in a pincer grasp position at the same time?
3. Were his motions smooth or did he pull and tug to get buttons through buttonhole?
4. How long did it take before the child was consistently successful?

Materials and Equipment

Chair appropriate to child's size
Chair for adult that brings him to eye level with child
Shirt with large buttons and buttonholes; buttons should be on right side of shirt

Instructional Objective

To have child button shirt independently.

Readiness

Pincer grasp.
Directs arm movements.
Directs hand movements.
Can alternate pincer grasp to left and right hand.

Procedure

1. Seat child on chair.
2. Sit on chair.
3. Place shirt with large buttons on right side on child.
4. Work on middle button with child; this is easily accessible to him.
5. Leave middle button completely unbuttoned.
6. Give child the command, (name), button your shirt!

7. Instruct child to pincer grasp button with right hand and side of shirt by buttonhole with left hand.

8. Direct him to push button half way through buttonhole with right hand and then grasp it with left hand in pincer grasp and pull it the rest of the way through and into proper position.

9. Repeat steps 5 through 8 until the child is consistently successful.

Task Evaluation

1. Did child maintain good grasp on buttons?

2. Could he use both hands in a pincer grasp position at the same time?

3. Were his motions smooth or did he pull and tug to get buttons through buttonholes?

4. How long did it take before the child was consistently successful?

Materials and Equipment

Chair appropriate to child's size

Chair for adult that brings him to eye level with child

Shirt with large buttons and buttonholes; buttons should be on right side of shirt

UNIT IV

LANGUAGE READINESS DEVELOPMENT

Figure 40

Competency Checklist

Name _____   Educational Facility _____

Date _____   Educator _____

Instructional Unit
Language Readiness Development

Code:

0 No Competency

1 Moderate Competency

2. Complete Competency

.... 1. Attends to adult when being spoken to.

.... 2. Extends tongue straight out when stimulated.

.... 3. Removes food particle from between lip and lower front teeth.

.... 4. Directs tongue to side of cheek to remove food.

.... 5. Directs tongue to lick food from outside of mouth.

.... 6. Responds verbally to stimulation.

.... 7. Imitates simple gestures.

.... 8. Imitates sounds.

.... 9. Responds to commands.

.... Total (Max. 18)

Remarks:

Instructional Objective

To have child attend to adult when being spoken to.

Readiness

Hearing is adequate.

Sight is adequate.

Directs head movement.

Directs eye movement.

Procedure

1. Initiate work with child in a room free of distractions.
2. If child is able to sit, place him on a small chair and sit opposite him. If he is not able to sit, lay him on his back and stand over him.
3. Give the child the command, (name), look at me!
4. Repeat this several times. Reward the child each time he looks at you.
5. Initially work face to face with child, but gradually move farther away from him demanding more attention each time he is given the command.

Task Evaluation

1. Did child immediately look at the adult when given the command?
2. Did he merely respond to the verbal stimulation or did he seem as though he recognized his name?
3. Did child attend for the entire time?

Materials and Equipment

Chair appropriate size for child
Chair for adult that brings him to eye level with child
Appropriate reward

Instructional Objective

To have child extend tongue straight out when stimulated.

Readiness

Sight is adequate.
Opens and closes mouth voluntarily.
Responds to taste stimulation.

Procedure

1. Seat child on chair using support if necessary.
2. Secure a tongue depressor and put a small amount of pudding or food on the end.
3. Give the child a small taste of the food.
4. Hold tongue depressor with food near the child's mouth. Food should be near enough to be obtained by extending the tongue.
5. Repeat the task several times until tongue extension is constantly achieved.

Task Evaluation

1. Did the child seem to realize after given the first taste of food that he could obtain a second taste by extending his tongue?
2. Did he extend his tongue far enough to reach the food?
3. Did he consistently extend his tongue to obtain the food?

Materials and Equipment

Chair appropriate size for child
Tongue depressors
Pudding

Instructional Objective

To have child develop skill in tongue movement by removing food from between lip and lower front teeth.

Readiness

Opens and closes mouth voluntarily.
Directs tongue movements.

Procedure

1. Seat child on chair using support if necessary.
2. Take a piece of sugar-coated cereal and place it in the child's mouth between lower front teeth and lower lip.

3. Hand child a mirror or place his chair so that he is sitting in front of a mirror.

4. Standing behind the child, focus the mirror so he can see the instructor demonstrate the task of removing a piece of cereal with the tip of the tongue.

5. If he does not respond to your demonstration, touch the tip of his tongue with your finger. He will bring it down in response to the touch.

6. Repeat the exercise often until the child becomes adequate in manipulating his tongue.

Task Evaluation

1. Did child become irritated when the cereal was placed in his mouth?

2. Did he imitate the instructor's movements?

3. Did he move his tongue down when stimulated by the instructor's touch?

4. Was he interested in watching himself in the mirror?

Materials and Equipment

Chair appropriate size for child
Mirror—hand or wall
Sugar-coated cereal

Instructional Objective

To have child develop skill in tongue movement by removing food from inside cheek.

Readiness

Opens and closes mouth voluntarily.
Directs tongue movements.

Procedure

1. Place the child in a sitting position; support him if necessary.

2. Secure a tongue depressor and place peanut butter on the end of it.

3. With the tongue depressor place the peanut butter inside the child's mouth on either the right or left cheek.

4. If child does not try to remove the peanut butter by manipulating his tongue to his cheek, assist him by guiding the tongue with the tongue depressor.

5. To guide the tongue, simply touch it with the tongue depressor on the side that is opposite the way you want it to go.

6. Assist the child with the tongue depressor until he initiates the movement on his own.

Task Evaluation

1. Did the peanut butter in the child's mouth irritate him immensely?

2. Did the tongue depressor irritate him?

3. Did he initiate any movement on his own to remove the peanut butter?

4. Did the guiding of his tongue with the tongue depressor initially communicate to him what he was to do?

Materials and Equipment

Chair appropriate size for child
Tongue depressor
Peanut butter

Instructional Objective

To develop essential skills in manipulating jaw and tongue muscles necessary for speech.

Readiness

Opens and closes mouth voluntarily.
Directs tongue movements.

Procedure

1. Seat child on chair using support if necessary.
2. With tongue depressor or index finger, spread a moderate amount of peanut butter or jelly around the outer perimeter of the lips.
3. Place him in front of a mirror.
4. Standing behind the child, demonstrate by doing the action that you want him to stretch his tongue out and lick the peanut butter or jelly off the outside of the lips.
5. If he does not imitate your motion, you may stimulate him to bring his tongue out of his mouth by touching it with a tongue depressor or by giving him a small taste of what is around his mouth.
6. Encourage him to move his tongue all around the outside of the lips, thus developing the mobility of the tongue.

Task Evaluation

1. Did child become irritated when the jelly or peanut butter was spread around the outside of the lips?
2. Did he imitate the instructor's movements?
3. Was he interested in watching himself in the mirror?
4. Did he stick his tongue out when stimulated by the tongue depressor or food?

Materials and Equipment

Chair appropriate size for child
Mirror—hand or wall
Peanut butter
Jelly
Tongue depressor

Instructional Objective

To have child respond verbally to stimulation.

Readiness

Sense to be stimulated is physically intact. (Such as hearing, feeling, sight.)
Makes cooing or babbling sounds.
Can voluntarily make sounds.

Procedure

1. Gather objects that stimulate the senses such as bells, flashlights and brushes.
2. Position child in most appropriate manner for desired stimulation activity.
3. Take a bell and ring it near the child's ear, talk to him and laugh out loud while doing it.
4. If the child coos, babbles or laughs when being stimulated, reward him.
5. It may be necessary to try a few activities before you find one that the child really enjoys.
6. Stimulation such as brushing or rubbing the child's body may prove to be just as exciting to him.

Task Evaluation

1. Did child seem annoyed by the stimulation?
2. Did he attend to the adult while working with him?
3. Did he seem to realize that he was being rewarded for verbally responding to the adult?
4. When stimulated a second and third time did he make the same sound?

Materials and Equipment

Chair appropriate size for child
Materials for stimulation such as:
    Bell, flashlight, brush

Instructional Objective

To have child imitate simple gestures: (bye, bye and hi).

Readiness

Directs arm and hand movements.
Babbles several sounds.
Attends to and turns to spoken voices.

Procedure

1. Begin to build a repertoire of communication by gesturing to the child to communicate everyday activities, bye, bye and hi.

2. Whenever the opportunity arises, such as leaving the child, gesture and say bye, bye.

3. Reward the child for every attempt to gesture or verbalize a need.

4. An important task on the part of the instructor is to observe carefully any movement that the child makes consistently when an activity occurs, and then make this movement during the same activity while verbalizing the appropriate word.

Task Evaluation

1. Did you notice that the child made any movement or babbling sounds before such activities as going some place, eating, going to the bathroom?

2. If the child did make any gesture was it appropriate for the activity such as waving before going out or holding himself in the area of the genitals before going to the bathroom?

3. Did the child seem to associate the words said to him with his gesture?

4. Did child try to gesture and verbalize the appropriate word in imitation of the adult?

Materials and Equipment

Chair appropriate size for child
Chair for adult that brings him to eye level with the instructor
Baby doll or any other object that the child may be able to verbalize the sound of

Instructional Objective

To have child imitate sounds.

Readiness

Attends to adult.
Reacts to noises.
Vocalizes sounds.

Procedure

1. Seat child on chair.
2. Sit on chair.
3. While holding a baby doll or some other familiar object, repeat the word baby or other appropriate names several times. While repeating, show the object to the child.
4. Reward the child appropriately for an approximation of the word.
5. When the child makes an attempt at the word, try and build a communication repertoire with him, by repeating the sounds that he made and then rewarding him if he makes it back; by doing this you are building communications with him.

Task Evaluation

1. Did the child attend to the adult when speaking to him?
2. Did he seem to associate the word with the object?
3. Did he made any attempt to verbalize in response to the adult?
4. Did he repeat the sound that he initially made when the adult made it?

Materials and Equipment

Chair appropriate size for child
Chair for adult that brings him to eye level with the instructor
Baby doll or any other object that the child may be able to verbalize the sound of

Instructional Objective

To have child respond to simple verbal commands.

Readiness

Vision is adequate.
Hearing is adequate.
Directs body movements.
Attends to adult.
Vocalizes voluntarily.

Procedure

1. The object of this exercise is to build, by imitation, the child's response to gestures and verbalizations. This can be done while working with two or three children. If working with more than one child, make sure that they are congenial and not distracting to each other.

2. Sit with the children and make sure that all children can see you.

3. Begin by requesting that the children attend to you. Reward each child who attends to you. Ignore those who do not attend.

4. When you have each child's attention, begin a *do this game.*

5. Start the game with a simple gesture such as a wave and the command, (name), do this! Reward each child who imitates the task. Repeat the command and gesture.

6. When each child has successfully imitated the gesture begin to use other gestures. Repeat until the child is consistently successful.

7. Next, begin to work on verbalizations by starting with simple words such as ma, ma. Give the command, (name), say ma, ma! Repeat until the child is consistently successful.

8. Reward each verbalization made by the child. Add words to increase the child's verbalization.

Task Evaluation

1. Did the child attend to you?
2. Did the child realize that he was being rewarded for imitating your actions or words?

3. Did the child achieve any imitations or verbalizations on a consistent basis?

Materials and Equipment

Chair appropriate size for the child
Chair for adult

APPENDIX
SUGGESTED RESOURCE MATERIALS AND EQUIPMENT
WITH ADDRESSES

Binky Baby Products, Inc.
New York, N.Y. 10010

Plastic coated spoon
Trainer cup

Childcraft Education Corp.
964 Third Avenue
New York, N.Y. 10022

Playtentials

Constructive Playthings
1040 East 85th Street
Kansas City, Mo. 64131

Unbreakable metal mirror

Creative Playthings
Princeton, N.J. 08540

Activator pulling sounds
Infant chimes mobile
Rainbow twirler

European Folk Craft Shop
525 Linden Street
Scranton, Pa. 18503

Big beach ball
Prone board

Invalex Company
741 West 17th Street
Long Beach, Calif. 90813

Potty chair

Oster Corporation
Milwaukee, Wis. 53217

Infra-red heat massager

J. T. Posey
39 S. Santa Anita Avenue
Pasadena, Calif. 91107

Posey restraint

J. A. Preston Corporation
71 5th Avenue
New York, N.Y. 10003

Large handled therapy spoon
Large handled therapy fork
Plate guard
Therapy chair

227

Sip'n' Spin, Inc.   Drinking cup
Irvington, N.J. 07111

Skill Development Equipment   Fa-t mat (wedge)
   Co.   Foam builder mat
1340 North Jefferson   Odd ball saddle
Anaheim, Calif. 92806

INDEX

A

Action-oriented programs, 8
Activities of daily living, 11
Adaptive behavior, 3
American Association on Mental Deficiency, 3
Attending, 215

B

Bar graph, 10
Bathing, 89
Bathroom, use of, 112-125
Behavior charting procedures, 10
Behavior reporting, 10
Behavioral competencies, 9
Bladder control, 118 (*see* Toileting)
Body manipulation, 19-20
Body rolling, 20
Bowel movement, 14
Brushes, variety of, 22-23

C

Changes, behavioral, 10
Charts
  curriculum, 10-11
  happenings, 15
  individual prescription, 11-12
  toilet training, 14
  visual representation, 10
Chewing, skill of, 12
  chopped food, reclining, 75
  chopped food, sitting, 74
Chewing process, alternate, 74
Child
  athetoid, 55
  floppy, 60
  nonambulatory, 20
  spastic, 55, 57
Circulatory process, 19
Clothing, care of, 122

Coat, skills of
  putting on, 189-193
  removal, 187-188
  unzipping, 199-201
  zipping, 202-205
Competency checklist, explanation of, 10, 19
  code, 19, 35, 63, 88, 98, 105, 112, 126, 215
  language readiness development, 215
  motor development, 35
  self-care development
    dressing, 126-129
    feeding and drinking, 63
    nasal hygiene, 98-99
    oral hygiene, 105
    toilet training, 112
    washing and bathing, 63
  sensory development, 35
Convex, 58
Crawling, 48-49
Creeping, 49-50
Cup, trainer, 70
Cup, holding, 84
  independent drinking from, 84
Curriculum, use of, 7
  chart, 10-11
  objectives, 7
  planning, 7-8, 10

D

Daily encounter report, 11
Developmental areas, 8
Developmental behavior, 10
Directed body movements, 19
Dressing, skill of, 129-213
Drinking, skill of
  from trainer cup, 70
  independent, 86
  through straw, 70

229

E

Eating, skill of
bite size food, 78
chopped food, 75
pureed food, 69
Eating utensils, skill of manipulating
fork, 85
knife, 87
spoon, 82
Education, public, 5
Educational encounter reporting, 11
daily, 13
procedures, 13
recommendations, 13
results, 13
weekly, 13-14
general procedures, 13
general results, 13-14
recommendations, 14
specific notable events, 14
Educational program, 7, 11
Elimination control, 14

F

Feeding, skill of
bottle, 67
dropper, 64
finger, 78
hand over hand method, 79-80

G

Gestures, imitation of, 222
Glass, skill of using
drinking from independently, 86
plastic "sip 'n spin," 71-72
Grasp, 14
Grooming (*see* Washing)

H

Hand over hand feeding method, 79-80
Hand over hand holding, 81
Hand over hand method, 110, 137-139,
142-143, 145-146, 148-151, 155-158,
160-161, 166-167
Hat, skills of
putting on, 179-180
removal, 175-178
Head balance, 37, 48

Head control
lifting, 36
of spastic and athetoid, 60
Hip rotation, 58

I

Imitation, method of, 7
Independent behavior skills
dressing
coat, putting on, 189-193
coat removal, 187-188
coat, unzipping, 199-201
coat, zipping, 202-205
cup drinking, 70
cup holding, 81
hat, putting on, 178
hat removal, 175
mitten, putting on, 186
mitten removal, 181
pants, putting on, 148-153
pants removal, 142-147
pants snapping, 196-198
pants unsnapping, 194-196
shirt buttoning, 208-213
shirt, putting on, 161-166
shirt removal, 154-161
shirt unbuttoning, 206-208
shoe, putting on, 171-174
shoe removal, 167-170
sock, putting on, 135-140
sock removal, 129-134
Individual prescription chart, 11, 12
Instructional unit
dressing
instructional objective, 129-131, 133-
136, 138-140, 143-145, 147-149,
151-157, 159-168, 170-184, 186-
189, 191-192, 194-197, 199-205,
206-210, 212
materials and equipment, 130-137,
139-141, 143-145, 147-168, 170-
184, 186-188, 190-205, 207-210,
212-213
procedure, 130-184, 186-189, 191-123
readiness, 129-140, 142-144, 146-153,
155-157, 159-164, 166-168, 170-
184, 186-189, 191-197, 199-210,
212

task evaluation, 130-142, 144-151, 153-185, 186-189, 191-210, 212-213

language readiness development
  instructional objective, 215-220, 222-224
  materials and equipment, 216-223, 225
  procedure, 216-224
  readiness, 215-219, 221-224
  task evaluation, 216-225

motor development
  instructional objective, 35-36, 38-40, 42-44, 46, 48-49, 51-52, 54-57, 59-60
  materials and equipment, 36, 38-44, 46-47, 50-51, 53-54, 56-57, 59-61
  procedure, 36-60
  readiness, 35, 37-39, 41-42, 45-46, 48-49, 51-52, 54-57, 59-60
  task evaluation, 36-37, 39-41, 43-44, 46-47, 49-57, 59-61

nasal hygiene
  instructional objective, 99-103
  materials and equipment, 100-104
  procedure, 99-104
  readiness, 99-102, 104
  task evaluation, 100-104

oral hygiene
  instructional objective, 105-107, 109, 111
  materials and equipment, 106-107, 109-110, 112
  procedure, 106-111
  readiness, 105-106, 108-109, 111
  task evaluation, 106-110

self feeding and drinking, 63
  instructional objective, 64-67, 69-70, 72, 74-75, 77-79, 81-87, 89
  materials and equipment, 64-67, 69-70, 72, 74-75, 77-79, 81-88
  procedure, 64-71, 73-74, 76-85, 87-89
  readiness, 64-65, 67, 69-72, 74, 76-79, 81-85, 87, 89
  task evaluation, 64-65, 66-70, 72, 74-75, 77-79, 81-88

sensory development
  instructional objective, 19-20, 21-24, 26-29, 31-32
    materials and equipment, 20-24, 26-33
    procedure, 20-32
    readiness, 19-24, 26-29, 31-32
    task evaluation, 20-31, 33

toilet training
  instructional objective, 113-116, 118-120, 122-124
  materials and equipment, 114-116, 118-120, 122-125
  procedure, 113-125
  readiness, 113-116, 118-119, 121-125
  task evaluation, 114-117, 119-121, 123-125

washing and bathing
  instructional objective, 90-93, 95-97
  procedure, 90-97
  materials and equipment, 90-98
  readiness, 90-92, 94-97
  task evaluation, 90-96, 98

Instructional objective, 8, 19
Instructional unit, explanation of, 19
Intellectual functioning, subaverage, 3
Intelligence quotient, 3
Intelligence scale, 3

K

Knife, use of, 87

L

Language readiness development, 215
Law in Pennsylvania, 5
Learning environment, 15
Learning sequence, 7
Limbs
  paralyzed, 21
  spastic, 21, 22
  tensing of, 21

M

Mental retardation
  care of, 4
  characteristics of severe and profound, 3, 4
  diagnosis of, 3
  history of education, 4

N

Nasal hygiene, 99-100, 102-103
National Association for Retarded Children, 5

O

Objectives, curriculum, 7
Odors, discrimination of, 31
Oral hygiene, 105-107, 109, 111

P

Pants, skills of
  putting on independently, 153
  removal independently, 147
  snapping, 196-198
  unsnapping, 194-196
Pelvic bone, 58
Pennsylvania State law, 5
Pincer grasp, 183-184, 186, 194-212
Pincer movement, 78
Plastic glass (*see* Glass)
Posey restraint, 24, 41
Posture, stabilized, 55, 57
Positions
  bent knee, 43
  crawling, 48
  kneeling, 45, 49
  knee-walking, 45
  prone on stomach, 37
  raised upper torso, 39
  side sitting, 56
  sitting, 43
  sitting with support, 40, 56
  stabilized, 55
  standing with support, 44-47
Potty chair, 115
Prescription, 11
Procedures, explanation of, 8-9
  diagnostic, 10
  prognostic, 10
  step-by-step, 11
Physical impairment, 19
Physical therapist, 55

R

Reaching, skill of, 39
Readiness, explanation of, 8-9

Reflex
  rooting, 22
  sucking, 22, 67
Relaxation of spasticity, 57, 59
Reporting of, educational encounter, 13
Response, verbal, 224
Rib hump, 58
Rolling, skill of, 42

S

Self-care development, skills of
  dressing, 129-213
  drying, 95-97
  drinking, 67, 70-72, 81-82, 84-85
  feeding, 64-67, 78-70, 73-81, 83-84, 85-88
  toileting, 112-125
Sensory development, 19
Severe and profound mental retardation, characteristics of, 3-4
Shirt, skill of
  putting on, 161-167
  removal of, 154-161
Shoes, skill of
  putting on, 171-175
  removal, 167-171
Skills, development of, 7
Sock, skill of
  putting on, 135-141
  removal, 129-135
Sound, skills of
  babbling, 8, 221
  cooing, 8, 221
  imitation of, 7, 223
Stimulation
  auditory, 19, 28
  olfactory, 19, 31
  sound, 35
  tactile, 19-29
  taste, 19, 32
  visual, 19, 29
Sucking response, 70
Sucking, skill of, 65
Sucking spout, 47
Support board, 47
Swallowing skill of, 65

T

Tactile stimulation, 19-29
Task evaluation, explanation of, 8
Task performance, explanation of, 7
Therapy spoon, 13, 82
Tongue
  root of, 66, 68-69, 73
Tongue control, language development
  movement, skill of, 216-218
Toileting, skill of, 112-125
Toilet training, 113
  charting, 113
  scheduling, 113

U

Uneducable, concept of, 5

W

Walking, skill of
  sideways, 51
  up steps, 54
  with assistance, 52
Walking pattern, alternating, 52
Washing, grooming, 89-98

Z

Zero reject system, 5

Units of instruction, 8
  language, 8
  motor, 8
  self-care, 8
  sensory, 8